MW00414537

BOOKS
GROW
BUSINESS

LEAD YOUR FIELD FAST AS AN AUTHOR
WITHOUT WRITING A SINGLE WORD

MARK IMPERIAL

with SHANNON BURITZ

Books Grow Business/ Mark Imperial -- 1st ed.
Chief Editor/ Shannon Buritz

ISBN: 978-1-954757-28-8

The Publisher has strived to be as accurate and complete as possible in the creation of this book.

This book is not intended for use as a legal, business, accounting, or financial advice source. All readers are advised to seek the services of competent professionals in legal, business, accounting, and finance fields.

Like anything else in life, there are no guarantees of income or results in practical advice books. Readers are cautioned to rely on their judgment about their individual circumstances to act accordingly.

While all attempts have been made to verify information provided in this publication, the Publisher assumes no responsibility for errors, omissions, or contrary interpretation of the subject matter herein. Any perceived slights of specific persons, peoples, or organizations are unintentional.

To Shannon, Max and Felix, Kaprice,
and Gammy and Gampy.

Contents

Foreword By Perry Marshall

My name is Perry Marshall. I'm the author of ten books. Today I'm well-known in several fields, including marketing, evolution, communication technology, and cancer research. I'd like to tell you a very embarrassing story about a failed attempt to achieve notoriety.

Seventeen years ago, some friends and I collectively agreed we all deserved to have Wikipedia pages. We correctly guessed that such an asset would enhance our personal credibility. So we wrote pages for each other.

We quickly found out we had no idea what we had gotten ourselves into. Two days later, my page got slapped with a fat banner across the top: "This appears to be a vanity page about a non-notable person. Please supply adequate references, or this page will be deleted."

The funny thing was, even back then, I was not a "nobody." I was well known in certain circles, selling a successful ebook and regularly getting asked to speak at seminars around the world.

But upon closer examination, I discovered that **zero** of my professional accomplishments were considered legit by Wikipedia's conventional standards of "notability." I could not point to any meaningful exposure in established media outlets. Nor any other credibility outside a couple of very narrow professional tribes I belonged to.

From the standpoint of the wider world, I was a nobody. A few days later, my page got taken down.

Fortunately, that was all the wake-up call I needed. I realized that all my credibility was built on a paper-thin and fickle role in a rapidly changing marketing scene. And that my success might be very short-lived if I didn't make an effort to establish lasting credibility and authority.

It only took a few conversations for me to conclude that I absolutely positively had to write a traditional, paper-and-ink book. I did so. That book was *Ultimate Guide to Google AdWords*, now in its 6th edition. It has sold 100,00 copies.

As a marketing consultant and advertising expert, I can assure you that the whims and rules, and dictates of social media and ad platforms change hourly… and in the midst of that tumult, selling books has been my #1 most reliable source of quality customers over the last seventeen years.

My decision to move my expertise from online-only to traditional paper and ink may be the biggest reason I'm still around. I'm not exaggerating.

A few years later, I felt I had some important things to say in science and evolutionary biology. There were many things I hoped to do that I didn't know how to do. But the ONE thing I absolutely needed to do, that I could do, was write a book. That book is now called *Evolution 2.0*.

The reason books are such a great way to attract customers is: Readers are leaders. It sounds trite, but it's true. A person who cracks a book, sits down and reads it, and learns from you is the highest quality client you can get without expending manual labor (doing things like getting on planes and speaking at conferences - those things are effective but not scalable).

(I also now have a legit Wikipedia page).

In *Books Grow Business*, Mark Imperial delivers a guide to writing and publishing books that not only gives you a solid start but explores a number of lesser-known strategies to market, distribute and "viralize" your book. Take his words seriously.

Perry Marshall, Author
Ultimate Guide to Google Ads
80/20 Sales & Marketing
Evolution 2.0

Introduction

Suppose you run a business or are planning to start a business and picked up this book. In that case, you are probably a published author or aspire to be one because you've somehow discovered the insider secret that books are the #1 solution for business development in any field. The evidence is all around you that the top earners in every field use a book as the nucleus of their business, including folks like Dr. Phil, Suze Ormond, and Dave Ramsey, to name a few. Even if you are shy and don't want to be "famous," you can become a recognized and respected name in your field without being a celebrity. Having a book allows you to help more people at a higher level and earn a more substantial income while working less so you can have the freedom to live your life.

I'm glad you are here. It is a shame that too many professionals struggle their entire careers because they don't have the status and differentiating power of a book. In contrast, others who know the secret create their books easily and climb to the top of their fields at blazing speed. Now you'll know the secrets.

If you've ever wondered if a book is a valuable marketing asset, Dan Kennedy says, "Nothing is more powerful for building instant credibility and authority than authorship." Russell Brunson says, "Authoring a book is the number one marketing asset that lives the longest." Your book is the atomic bomb of business cards. It doesn't just define you; it memorializes you in the mind of your market.

After all, it's practically a sin to throw away a book. While business cards are tossed out almost as quickly as they are handed out, your book will likely be read, loaned out, and live on someone's bookshelf forever.

How much is a client worth to you? $1,000? $5,000? $10,000? Since your book can send your perfect message to the masses without your time, you only need to attract 100, 500, or 1,000 people to reach one million dollars. It's easier than you may think. Some folks I know do that monthly with their book.

If you've put off having this asset in your business, it's not your fault. There are so many talking heads trying to sell you every advertising solution on the planet; it's no wonder everyone is confused.

If you ever worried you didn't know what to write about or were insecure about your ability to write, this book will show you exactly how to turn your knowledge into a client-attracting book and even how to find a professional to help you ensure your book is well-written if you don't want to write it yourself.

Business owners waste millions of dollars on ads that don't ever recover their costs due to predatory salespeople who are always targeting them with advertising offers, whether they are appropriate for the business or not. This noise distracts from getting foundational assets done, like a book.

Once you read this book, you will have a clear picture of how your book becomes the nucleus of your business. Then, you'll be able to make informed decisions on which advertising media makes sense and just say "NO!" to the predatory salespeople once and for all.

They say, "Build it, and they will come," but they left out the important part: "*if you know how to get the word out.*" Too many business owners I speak to say they get their business through word-of-mouth or referrals. When I hear that, I know it means they live beneath their calling because they don't understand marketing. Building it without effectively getting the word out is like building a storefront in the middle of the desert that most people will never see. One of the best ways to quickly, effectively, and efficiently get your word out is by authoring your own book.

If you're considering authoring a book, you may have many questions such as...

"How can authoring a book be the solution to my business growth?"

"Why should authoring a book be the FIRST thing I do to grow my business?" (The answer may surprise you)

"How am I qualified to have a book? What would I talk about?"

"This sounds hard; how much time does it take to write a book?"

"Once I've authored my book, how exactly do I use it to grow my business?"

You're not alone. Over the last 22 years, I've helped hundreds of business owners dramatically grow their businesses while decreasing their workload. I've realized that there are many ways to promote a business. However, each method will vary in efficiency and effectiveness. Nothing is a more direct path to success and growth than authoring the right kind of book for your field. Note that I said "the right kind of book," which is what *this* book will show you.

It's no secret that being recognized as an expert authority gives you a substantial advantage over your competition. Authoring a book is the #1 fastest and most definitive way to establish yourself as an expert authority in your field. Researchers at Pew Research and Publisher's Weekly recently reported that in 2022, people are reading more than ever. In the top 5 categories is Business & Money, so there's never been a better time to author a book in your field.

In this book, I'll let you in on the little-known secrets of how busy professionals and celebrities get their books done with maximum effectiveness in minimum time. You can have your book done in a matter of weeks, not years. In fact, you would find that the longer you work on your book, the more it will sabotage your success and happiness with the result! I'll even show you solid books that can be created in less than an hour. I will debunk the myths around books and demystify the book creation process that prevents people from considering authoring a book, keeping them at bay, believing it is beyond their ability or entitlement (this is to your advantage!)

With your authored book, you will gain the same category leader benefits as famous people like Dave Ramsey, Suze Ormond, and Dr. Phil, just to name a few. Even if you don't want to be a famous name, you can be a humble authority and reap the same rewards. One thing in common with every widely known business celebrity is that they are all published authors. This is no coincidence; this is the nucleus of their personal brand marketing. It is a little-discussed secret hidden in plain sight. Why do they author books? (Many of them don't even "write" them). The many reasons will become clear as this book unfolds.

In this book, I'll show you how authoring a book will put your business development on steroids.

Mark Imperial mastering Influential Writing with Dan Kennedy during The No BS Independent Business Advisor Certification

Inside this book, you'll discover...

- How authoring a book instantly puts you in the Top 1% of the population by doing one thing that most of your competition will never conceive is achievable. This book will show you how authoring a book is more accessible than most people think.
- How a book provides the busy consumer a "shortcut" to recognizing YOU as the leader in the field so they can put you at the top of their list. A book is the quickest identifier for your prospects to know who you are and exactly how you can help them.
- How a book gives you instant Authority, Expert Credibility, and Celebrity status in your field. Don't worry; even if you are shy, you can do this as a humble authority.
- How your book delivers you the highest quality clients. You will discover that your best, most compliant, and highest paying clients will come from your book.
- How a book transforms you from an ordinary salesperson to an authority, educator, and advocate for your client's success. This positions you at the top of your field and separates you from your competition fast and forever.
- How to use your book as the ultimate lead generation tool for attracting an endless stream of highly qualified prospects that you can nurture to become your clients.
- How to be INVITED to speak to groups of your perfect prospects. Books open doors otherwise unattainable.
- How to appear on TV, Radio, Magazines, and other news media using your book.
- How to use your book as the ultimate referral tool and establish all the referral partners you want..
- How your book becomes the NUCLEUS of your content marketing and your "playbook," making your weekly outreach topics a breeze.

- How your book can bring you millions of dollars, delivering your perfect pitch while you sleep.
- How to author a book with your knowledge, ideas, and personality without writing a single word in as little as one hour. I'm not kidding; just wait until you discover this method.

Starting, growing, and scaling a business or professional practice can be overwhelming. But it doesn't have to be. It can be a breeze when you have the powerful advantage of a book as the nucleus of your business development.

I've seen many people make costly mistakes and waste a ton of time writing a book the old-fashioned way. That could have easily been avoided if they just had the right information and answers to their questions.

That's why I wrote this book – to help you navigate the business-growing book maze and have a solid action plan for growing and scaling your business or professional practice or starting a brand new business using the client/customer-getting power of a book.

No fluff, only straight information you want to know and NEED to know before you spend another minute or another dollar trying to promote your business without the advantages of a book. I'll cover the benefits, pros, and cons and answer the most pressing questions I get about authoring a book to grow your business. I'll also dispel the biggest myths and misconceptions around the creation and use of books in marketing and share the most common mistakes people make and how to avoid them.

Let me be clear. While this book is packed with valuable information about the most common issues you may face, it doesn't have all the answers. That would be impossible because there is no single right answer for everyone.

Even though the differences may be small, every situation is unique. So, if you have a question or concern not addressed in this book, I'm here to help. You can reach my team and me for a complimentary Book Idea Action Plan Session at **www.booksgrowbusiness.com** or email us at **actionplan@booksgrowbusiness.com**.

To your success!
MARK IMPERIAL

Complimentary Book Discovery Session

Would you like **FREE** help with your book idea? Or do you need an idea for a book that will attract your ideal clients?

Schedule your complimentary, no-obligation 30-minute **"Book Discovery Session"** at the link below to connect with my team and me.

Together, we will explore your goals and ideas, and create a clear action plan to get an excellent book done fast that brings you the clients of your dreams.

Visit: www.BooksGrowBusiness.com

CHAPTER ONE

Why a Book Is the First Marketing Asset You Should Create

*"There is no more essential a tool of
authority than authorship."*
— Dan S. Kennedy, Millionaire Maker

B ooks are the most overlooked, best-kept secret to growing your business or personal brand. In today's trust-based economy, there's no greater tool for building trust than demonstrating your ability and willingness to help. A book is a perfect vehicle for this application.

A Book Helps People Quickly Understand and Recognize Who You Are

"Focus on the Who-ing more than the Do-ing." - Mark Imperial

Today people are busier than ever before. The commercial noise of advertising and marketing messages increases every single day.

People are overwhelmed with information, so they have been conditioned to look for shortcuts. Being the author of a book gives you the ultimate shortcut that helps people quickly understand who you are and what you're about. With a great title for your first signature book, people can recognize who you help and how you help them. If you're a business owner or self-employed professional, authoring a book should be your number one priority and tool in your "Prime Positioning Portfolio," as I refer to it.

What Is a Prime Positioning Portfolio?

Simply put, a Prime Positioning Portfolio is a collection of marketing assets you choreograph for prospects to discover and quickly recognize who you are, who you serve, and how you serve them. It should position you as a subject matter expert in the field. Correctly done, this should position you as the obvious expert. A book is the most powerful and versatile marketing asset in your Prime Positioning Portfolio. To fully explain its power, I'll give an example of how I discovered this portfolio.

Long ago (I'll date myself), in the 1980s, I was an aspiring disc jockey. The hobby was on the rise. I was just another dime-a-dozen DJ spinning tunes in their bedroom, and I needed a way to stand out. I was young, and at the time, there were teen clubs that we would frequent, where the DJ was the star, and everybody was on the dance floor. There were so few clubs in the area then, and hundreds of DJs were trying to get spots playing in those clubs. So what could I do to stand out? What I discovered changed my life forever.

As a DJ, I would play 12-inch dance records, many of them imported from Italy and all over Europe. Long story short, I found the equipment to make this electronic music and built my own studio in my bedroom. Along with a handful of fellow music fans, we started to imitate and recreate the records we were playing from Europe. You may or may not have heard of house music, but that is how it was born. I released one of Chicago's first known house music records in 1985. When I did this, I didn't look at it like a Prime Positioning Portfolio asset. I just thought I was having fun making music, doing something I was interested in, and maybe impressing some girls. But a really cool thing happened. My record started getting played by other DJs in teen clubs, at dances and parties, and on the popular hot mix shows on the radio. Well, you can imagine what happened next. Instead of applying to DJ at clubs, the clubs were calling *me.* And anywhere I wanted to play that didn't call me, I simply dropped off a record, and I was in. My friends started riding along on my coattails, and when I would get a spinning job, they would ask if they could carry my records and warm up the crowd for me.

Just like that, I discovered the power of a Prime Positioning Portfolio asset. In that case, it was a dance record. And for the rest of my professional career in that field and others, even when I took my nightclub DJ career to private parties, weddings, and corporate events, I used the business equivalent of that dance record, which is a book!

Later in life, when Dan Kennedy mentored me, this was validated when he publicly shared with me that "the higher up the income ladder you go in any industry, you will see that the highest paid folks are being paid for who they are, rather than what it is they do," because what they do is a commodity and who they are is an expert, authority, or celebrity. When I discovered this power and this shortcut, I decided the first thing I should do in any field I entered was create this essential Prime Positioning Portfolio asset - a book.

Your Book Memorializes Your Unique Methods and "Brands" You in the Mind

Your book is the most excellent way to anchor your values into the mind of your prospects. People can quickly recognize you and know what you are about and link you to something they perceive as novel, fresh, and proprietary. Something different that solves their problems better than any other option available to them.

Beto Perez wasn't the first person to teach Latin dance as a way to get in shape. But Beto Perez had the balls to formalize a handful of his trainings, give it the name "Zumba," and put it out to the world. The result? A company worth over $500 million. I probably don't have to ask you if you've heard of it.

You have a way of doing your work and serving your clients that you may never have considered documenting or formalizing. Tony Robbins could have been just another run-of-the-mill personal development speaker. To this day, people identify Tony as the creator of "Personal Power," the first book and training system I ever purchased from him. That book launched his career to astronomical proportions and anchored his name in the mind as "The Personal Power Guy." Whatever Tony does now, from retreats to Fiji or online coaching programs, when people hear his name, they know his program aims to improve lives.

You don't think you do anything special? Think again! Perhaps you think that just because you went to the same school as everyone else in your profession, you are not unique and do the same thing that everybody else does. That is simply impossible because we all grow up with different influences, beliefs, and a different set of mentors, with various tips, tricks, and secrets.

The one thing people cannot replace, even in a commodity field, is YOU. The greatest thing you can do to help people, including yourself, is formalize your methods, create a memorable name, and show the world who you are and what you do.

A Book Puts You in the Top 1% And Separates You From Your Competition

Because you've opened this book, I know you are a one-percenter. Very few people would even have the thought cross their minds of writing a book. As I write, I have been browsing Amazon in the wealth management category, and there are only around 8,000 titles. There are over 300,000 financial advisors. In the mortgage category on Amazon, there are only 5,000 titles, and there are over 400,000 mortgage loan originators. These statistics indicate that when you author a book, you're instantly in the top 1% to 3% of your field. Currently, statista.com reports that there are 49,000 authors in the United States, which would put you in the top .0001% of the U.S. population who are authors.

Due to the very nature of writing, it deters most of your competition from even bothering. Because so many won't even consider authorship, very few will discover the secrets in this book, and even fewer will understand the power and commit to having a book published in the next 90 days. No matter what field or industry you are in or who you serve, authoring a book in less than 90 days will make you stand out. There is no faster method to separate you from your competition and position you at the top of your field than a book.

You, a Published Author?

Another preconceived notion that works in your favor is that people believe there is some sort of qualification required to be an author. In my daily conversations with business owners, I often ask, "Have you been published? Do you have a book on your expertise?"

Often their responses range from "I've never considered it because I can't write" or "I've thought about it but have no idea what to do, so I dismissed it immediately" or "Me? I'm not better than anyone else so I can't call myself an expert; therefore I don't deserve to have a book." With those kinds of preconceived notions out there, it makes it easy for us to leapfrog to the top, where there is little competition!

The good news is that it is easier than they think, but we will keep that our little secret. Here is the reality: When we stop worrying about proving to people that we are the "expert" and just focus on actually *helping* them, it makes it easy for *them* to call us the "expert."

If you already sell your services or products through conversations with your prospects, either in person or by phone or email, then you already have what it takes to author your book. To take the mystery out of authorship, all you have to recognize is that the only thing authors do is transfer their knowledge into print. If you have the answers to your prospect's problems, you have specialized knowledge worthy of sharing in a book. You don't need to be the world's leading expert on your subject; you only need to be one step ahead of your readers, who will benefit from your book. The thought that you need to be the best before you author a book is precisely the thinking that will keep you from becoming the best. It is no secret that books are the vehicles that catapult people to the top of their field, so it is the other way around.

I grew up in martial arts with a black belt in Goju Shorei Karate. One of the conditions for earning your black belt includes mentoring and teaching others. This is because teaching leads to mastery. I found this accurate as I had to hone my skills and gain deep knowledge to transfer the skill to another person. I was expected to teach those who were not at my level and didn't have a black belt yet. I started teaching when I barely had my purple belt. The point is, you BEGIN teaching before you think you've "earned the right" to teach. Therefore, you earn the right to be called the "expert." Remember, being an "expert" isn't what you strive for; you strive to help others. By doing so, *they* will call you an "expert" as a byproduct.

Are you afraid you are not a good writer? Don't worry; in the later chapter on creating your book, you will see how you can enlist the help of a professional writer to transfer your knowledge into print. Are you afraid you're not sure what to write about? Again, don't worry because, in that specific chapter, I will show you how to come up with the most appealing topic and title for your book. And considering you know your craft, you already know how to answer your prospect's most burning questions.

If for any reason you've procrastinated creating your book, I give you permission to finally get it done. No excuses. Look at it as Version 1.0. It doesn't have to be perfect because there is no such thing. Authors commonly update their books with follow up "editions" so it is okay! After all, Windows 11 wouldn't have happened if Bill Gates didn't get version 1.0 out, so do it now!

You will hear an expression from me a lot: Readers are looking for answers, not advertising. Be the provider of those answers, and you will be seen as a trusted advisor, not a salesperson.

Your Best Clients Will Come From Your Book

My primary mentor taught me this, and I validated it in my own business. Dan Kennedy has publicly shared that over 65% of his members in his subscription membership business came from one person who read his book. And even more importantly, his highest-paying members and those who invested most prominently originated from book readers. And, even more importantly, his highest paying members and those who invested in his highest levels of investment were all from book readers.

This makes sense if you think about the essence of book seekers and readers. Look at Amazon.com, which is another search engine like Google. However, the difference is that the people USING Amazon.com to search are "buyers." They aren't looking for free information; instead, they are looking for a book to buy that will give them the knowledge they seek. While Google is used by everyone worldwide, most looking for instant (and free) answers, Amazon is browsed by folks wanting and expecting to buy something.

I would much rather get a buyer on my list than someone who took something for free, even if it is a low-priced buyer. I used to build lists from free report giveaways. That is okay, but a book buyer is even better because they prove their higher level of interest by making a small investment. Books are great because they serve your existing clients, customers, and audience, and because books are low-priced, they make low-risk purchases for cold traffic and audiences who do not yet know you. In summary, a book is an excellent filter to separate the better prospects from the suspects.

When I had my wedding DJ business, I wrote a book on wedding receptions and generously handed it out to prospects at bridal shows and any events I attended. I would mail my books to prospects. What I found was that my best clients came from those books. They accepted my higher premium fees more readily, and because my book intentionally but tactfully (sneakily) detailed the work involved, the readers invested in the highest level programs. Before reading my book, they had no frame of reference as to what "a DJ should cost," so any price quoted would sound expensive. On top of that, readers of my book made the best and most well-behaved clients. That's something that I certainly didn't expect. I mean that they would read the chapter about music requests from your DJ, and they would understand the methodology that songs are three to four minutes long, and an hour is 60 minutes. So I would train them only to request a fraction of that hour to allow the DJ to program properly. If you weren't aware, one of the biggest problems DJs face is the impossible request lists from brides and grooms. They have hundreds of songs that would require a week's worth of time to play. That always leads to a disappointed, disillusioned bride who says, "You didn't play any of my requests." When I educated couples about this simple fact in one of the chapters of my book, the results were mindblowing. They complied, became better clients for me, and were much more satisfied with the overall reception experience.

This isn't surprising, and here's why. Think about the nature of the typical "book reader." They are knowledge seekers who are already demonstrating that they're more invested in the success of whatever they're trying to do by researching and showing a willingness to learn and be coachable. This fact makes it very clear why your best clients will come from your book.

This Also Works to Attract Non-Readers

According to the U.S. Department of Education, reported by Forbes magazine, 54% of adults in the United States (130 million people) are less than proficient in literacy and read below the equivalent of a sixth-grade level. Even in the face of this statistic, you still gain considerable advantage by authoring a book because whether they read it or not, they still know you wrote the book on your subject matter. Even illiterate people will know Suze Orman, Dave Ramsey, or Dr. Phil, not just from their television or radio programs but their authored books, whether or not they have read them. You may agree that an author is held in high regard, whether you've read their work or not. "Author of the book _____" is often the introduction used to bring guests on many TV and radio talk shows. It is a powerful distinction that garners respect, even if the effect is implanted in the audience subliminally.

Books Last a Lifetime

There is no other marketing asset in your Prime Positioning Portfolio that will last longer than an authored book. Take advertisements, for example. They come and go. Television commercials air for 30 to 60 seconds, and they're gone. Direct mail pieces, newspapers, and magazine articles are all excellent assets, but they only last the lifetime of their publication frequency. Newspapers arrive daily before they get thrown in the trash or at the bottom of the birdcage. Magazines come weekly or monthly, and they're gone. Direct Mail gets sifted over a garbage can. There is a place for all of those things. But the point I want to convey is that your book, as a marketing asset, will last you a lifetime.

Dan Kennedy himself still lives off of his very first book, "The Ultimate Sales Letter," first published in 1990, separating him from all other copywriters in his field. In fact, he blazed the trail for copywriters, many starting in the profession after reading the book. All of that bolsters Dan's position as the top expert in the field. Dan has told us stories of how the book got him speaking engagements, hired personally, to train the entire staff of numerous companies. These companies would buy copies of the book for every person attending the meeting, even mandating that every employee read the book or be fired, as the man who wrote the book conducted the training session. Even today, 32 years later, people are quoting that book, recommending that book, and acknowledging Dan as the leader of his field by having authored that book. So what other evidence do you need regarding the power of books lasting a lifetime?

People Look For Answers, Not Advertising

When people face a life challenge, do they look for advertising? Watch commercials? No. Of course not. Those ads and commercials are ignored while they pick up a book. Almost every successful person, when interviewed, reveals being inspired by a book somewhere along the timeline of their life. In the business world, it may have been "The Art of War." Interestingly, this book is only 64 pages! So that shows you a book doesn't need to be long to be impactful! Another example is Napoleon Hill's "Think and Grow Rich." Regardless of the industry, many people have read "How to Win Friends and Influence People."

Books are anchored firmly in the human mind as helpful resources, making them widely accepted and desired. Books don't raise alarms like junk mail. Even with the popularity of webinars, most people's brains have been conditioned to file them under the category of "sales pitches." But preconceived notions about books are purely positive.

So unless you screw it up, you will have a powerful tool at your disposal. With this book as your guide, I will teach you how *not* to screw it up and how to create a welcomed and valuable resource that does not give off a "sales pitch in disguise" vibe. It's easy to ensure your book is received well. You just have to be conscious of its creation. Just avoid being too salesy and you'll be okay, especially in today's socially connected society where people will eagerly leave their negative reviews on Amazon about a book being "nothing but a sales pitch for the author." With this book's tips and guidelines, you will *only* provide what your readers are ultimately seeking - answers.

Duplicate Yourself

Many self-employed business owners and professionals sell one-to-one with face-to-face or Zoom meetings. With a book, you can give that perfect presentation every time, even if you are sleeping, on vacation, or playing golf. For every ten books I mail out to prospects, at least three become book clients. So it saves me the time of speaking to all ten people, and I can devote myself to the three who booked appointments and want to move forward. That conversation is typically based on which package or program is best for them, so they were pre-sold.

A book is scalable because you are only limited to the number of books you can mail out or that people find on Amazon to purchase. The potential is limitless. You can offer thousands of people a free digital copy of your book via email or social media advertising, whether Facebook, YouTube, or even LinkedIn.

Think about what a fantastic tool a book is. In one fell swoop, it not only defines who you are and positions you as the obvious expert, but it delivers value in the information you give out, instantly rewarding you with credibility and authority. I first stumbled across this power in 1994. It's a bizarre story.

I used to sell $1,500 in pet iguanas every Sunday. I had a table at a flea market here in the Chicagoland area just for fun because reptiles were a hobby of mine. I purchased iguanas in bulk from an importer in Florida. As you might imagine, many people were always gathered around my table, browsing and asking questions about these intriguing creatures. I began to get tired of repeating myself over and over again, so I decided to write a pamphlet entitled the "Iguana Island Care Guide." This guide outlined the benefits of having a pet iguana, their diet, how to care for them, what mistakes to avoid, and frequently asked questions. From then on, whenever I had swarms of people asking the same old questions, I slapped a copy of the guide into their hands. Let's be honest; I mostly did that out of laziness.

But then something amazing happened. The people I had given the pamphlets to would return that same day or the following Sunday, pamphlet in one hand, cash in the other to buy an iguana. Then they would also purchase all of the things they learned they needed from the guide, like calcium supplements and heat lamps. Not only did those little written pamphlets save my voice, but they also did all the selling for me. So I started barking, "Hey, come get your free Iguana Island Care Guide!" Before I knew it, I went from selling ten iguanas daily to 30 to 50 iguanas a day before noon! If a book works for selling iguanas, it will work for *any* business. I have yet to find a single market for which a book would not sell. And it's not just for the information itself because you gain positioning from being a published author on Amazon, whether people actually read the book or not.

A Book Allows People to Become Immersed in You

I jokingly call this artificially inseminating a relationship because folks that come to me after reading my book or consuming my materials have a very different demeanor. They approach me as a friend, as opposed to a salesperson. Their arms are not figuratively crossed in suspicion but instead eagerly wanting more of what I gave them. An early mentor taught me that people wouldn't open their wallets or give you a check until they give you their attention and time.

A book is a long-form way to get people immersed in you. And that's why we do content. Whether you're doing videos, blogs, or articles, a book is at the top of the food chain amongst all those pieces of content. Imagine somebody picking up your book daily, over a few days, and learning a little bit more about you and your methodology each time. Can you see how they are giving you their attention and getting closer to you? If you include personal anecdotes, examples, and stories, they are even more likely to resonate with you.

At the end of the day, people don't just hire you for what you do. They hire you for who you are. The "know, like, and trust" factor is vitally important. In your book, you'll be giving away some of your greatest advice and little-known tips, tricks, and secrets that very few talk about. Later in this book, I'll share with you precisely how to do this without giving away your secrets because, ultimately, the people looking to do it themselves would never hire you. Your client should be the person that wants it done for them, has more money than time, values their time, and wants someone else to take the burden off their shoulders. A book demonstrates your unique abilities and results without speaking with each prospect one-on-one.

Books build raving fans. That's why authors sign autographs. When was the last time a salesperson was asked for their autograph? Regarding immersion, books are kept as opposed to business cards that are thrown away or lost. Books are put on a shelf, passed around, or kept on a coffee table or desk. People refer to them. That's why I prefer physical books as opposed to digital ones.

By the way, your clients *want* you to succeed. They have a pride in hiring and they want to be known as working with the best. Even if you choose to be a humble expert, that is fine, but your clients will treat you like you're famous! A book allows you to choose the level of fame you want.

Having Your Own Published Book is Your Greatest Advantage Because Few People Have One

Studyfinds.org reports that more than half of Americans think they've got a good idea for a book, but most have never attempted to write one. In a survey of 2,000 people, 15% reported they had started writing a book, and only 6% had gotten halfway through. The most significant barrier reported was writer's block. But the lesser known barrier is referred to as "imposter syndrome." Most people feel they aren't qualified to write a book, so they don't even try.

Let's address that for a minute. Let me tell you why you *are* qualified to write a book. Are you already selling a product or a service to help people? Do you explain this product or service in face-to-face meetings or over the phone? If so, you're already qualified to write a book because you know more about that product or service than the person you're talking to. That's all you need to be able to do to express your knowledge in a book effectively. An author doesn't claim to be the "top expert" or "#1" in their field, but they offer a solution to a problem in a way that they find better. That is what makes each author unique. There is something that can't be duplicated: the individual writing the book with all of their distinctive qualities and experiences. I have a specific set of life experiences, along with a particular group of mentors I've chosen to learn from. You undoubtedly have an entirely different set of experiences and mentors. So the way that you and I see the world is totally different. However, we may solve the same problems, only with different solutions. That's why there are multiple authors on the same subject because the higher you go on the income ladder, the more people are hiring you for who you are and not for just the commodity of what it is you do.

A second big barrier to completing books is feeling like it is a monumental task. It's a misconception, and I can prove it to you. If you've listened to an audiobook, you'll notice that most of them are between two and six hours long. Imagine speaking to your clients. Do you have 30-minute or one-hour meetings? If you captured everything you said in those meetings, just think how quickly you would be able to create content for a book! Of course, it takes proper planning and organization of the information beforehand, but the point is that books are not as long and intimidating as they appear. For many of my clients, we have created books from existing material such as stage presentations, webinars, YouTube videos, or blogs. Books are not as complicated as people like to think. Let's keep that our little secret.

Another misconception is thinking you have to write the "A to Z" encyclopedia on your subject matter. This is actually the worst thing you can do. Instead, focus on one problem and one solution, which I will discuss in depth later.

Finally, people are deterred from authoring books because they think they need an agent and that they need to pitch the book to publishers. That's an old-fashioned way of thinking and only was a problem long ago when publishing was not accessible to mere mortals. Publishing houses were like gatekeepers. But that is no longer the case. With everything going to the web, all the tools you need to publish a book are at your disposal. Because of Amazon and other online booksellers, you don't need mass media distribution to have physical books in bookstores, similar to what happened in the music industry.

Anyone has access to becoming an author. However, the quality of your work matters, and the audience will be the judge. So just because anybody *can* become an author doesn't mean everyone will be a *great* author. It comes down to simply knowing your stuff, and if you don't consider yourself a writer, simply let a professional writer proofread and edit for you. Be good at what you do, and believe in educating and advocating for client success. Becoming a published author is accessible, which is excellent news because it's easy to leapfrog all those misconceptions and barriers in your mind that prevent you from getting it done.

Books Are the Foundation of Your Future Content

When you write a book, you are essentially designing your playbook for creating content for the entire year ahead. Each chapter can be broken into bullet points and subject matter for social media videos, as you'll be able to leverage your book content for all of your marketing, stage presentations, and speaking engagements. Books define who you are and who you stand for and against, allowing your readers to qualify you quickly. It's why a book is the first thing you should create, ignoring the marketing noise telling you to buy an ad first. A book instantly becomes the nucleus of your marketing. You will thrive on this book for years to come, if not your entire career.

CHAPTER TWO

The Five Trust Triggers: Turning Your Book Into Your #1 Trust-Building Asset

"People seek answers, not advertisements."
— *Mark Imperial*

B y default, your book will already be a respected and perceived resource. You can only do things to sabotage it. Your book's intention should be to inform and educate your audience while expressing your abilities, knowledge, and personality. Your reader will become comfortable knowing that you're the right person for them. You must have the right balance of information and empathy for your reader. In this chapter, you will discover what to include and what not to include to achieve the balance.

Books Are Viewed as a Respected Resource by Default

People all over the world respect books. Books are considered tools of scholars. In fact, books are so respected that CEOs and top executives of corporations are always itching to publish their own books. Once they become published authors, they know they will join the top one percent of experts and authorities in their field. CEOs and top executives are regarded as thought leaders, so much so that books are considered their legacy. People want to leave behind their life's work as a legacy.

This brings up another linked benefit to books. They are the longest-lasting marketing asset any business owner or professional can ever have. I advocate for people to create their books early in their careers. I noticed growth exploded in all my businesses once I published a book for each. After helping over 400 professionals get published, I thought it was about time to put THIS book together to show you the process, as I know it will only help me reach more business owners and professionals that need guidance with their book! But as the old saying goes, "Shoemaker's kids have no shoes."

I initially thought the first things I needed in my business were sales materials like letters or videos. I created DVDs, brochures, flyers, and postcards for each of my businesses. It's kind of funny to think about now, but all those sales materials are quickly discarded. Nobody is looking for sales materials. Anything that even resembles sales material gets tossed in the trash.

In contrast, your book is a whole different animal. People purchase books as gifts to give one another. They keep them on their bookshelves. They loan them out. You won't hear about people giving sales letters or webinars as gifts. Think about how those other materials are perceived and received. They automatically feel salesy. People expect a sales pitch in a webinar, seminar, luncheon, or free report, also known as a white paper.

Books not only transform your business. They transform who you are and how you are perceived. For example, people brag about knowing authors. People don't brag about knowing salespeople. Have you ever heard someone say, "Want to meet my friend? She sells mortgages!" Unlikely. It would be better if you heard, "Hey! Would you like to meet my friend? She is the author of "Mortgage for Mavericks."

People enjoy being brought into stories. If you invited a friend for lunch to meet the author of "Mortgage for Mavericks," they would undoubtedly be interested in finding out what the book was about. That is the essence of books. Books can quickly and easily define who you are and what you're about. They can transform you into an expert in your field.

For example, the question, "What's that book about?" further allows your DNA statement to come to light. If I haven't explained a DNA statement, I will cover that topic extensively in my other book, "Action Brand Marketing." Your "DNA statement" stands for "distinction of novel appeal." What makes you unique?

Here is an example of a DNA statement:

> "You know how tough it is for business owners and self-employed people to get loans? Well, this book includes tips, tricks, and secrets so those folks can not only get their own homes financed but also their investment properties. It's great for those who want to use their business to accumulate wealth through investment."

If I had to choose between sitting with that author or a salesperson at lunch, it would be easy to decide who would provide a more stimulating conversation.

Books Open Doors

When you create a book and give it the right title, it becomes a door opener. Books break through the noise. With so much advertising and marketing clamor, people ignore and discard marketing messages left and right. Your book, on the other hand, will stay on your prospect's desk. Want to reach a CEO guarded by a secretary behind closed doors and unreachable by telephone? Send them your book. If they're not automatically reaching out to you, your follow-up call has a greater chance of getting through when you're introduced as the author of the book you just sent.

Case Study: Adam

I'll give you an example. Adam Marburger is the owner of a thriving business in the automotive industry. His life and business were transformed once his book was released. Adam immediately sent copies of his book to the most influential people in his industry, including executives at NADA, the National Automobile Dealers' Association.

Every year when NADA chooses speakers for their conference, there are over 300 applicants for speaking opportunities. This year, because Adam's reputation preceded him through his book, his name not only stayed at the top of the pile but was chosen for his first five-figure speaking contract at what is considered the Super Bowl of automotive dealership events.

What doors do you want to be opened for you in your industry? What high-level organizations do you want to get attention from? Can you see how your book will help you do that?

Let's talk about what to include in your book. The five most essential elements are what I refer to as "trust triggers."

Trust Triggers

What are trust triggers? They are shortcuts and identifiers that build trust in the prospective reader. These trust triggers come in the form of teachings, lessons, demonstrations of your abilities, stories, educational case studies from actual clients, and discoveries — stories of things you've learned through either education or hard lessons.

Use the following five trust triggers throughout your book:

Trigger #1: Affinity

With affinity, consider the following questions your reader may be asking.

- Is this for me?
- Is the author familiar with my problem?

Although business is business, and for the most part, all have similar problems, business owners believe their issues are unique. They feel that nobody understands them. They want to know that the author of the book they're reading or the person they're considering working with understands. Trigger trust through affinity in your book's readers by using stories and case studies that relate to the most common scenarios regarding their problems.

Case Study: The Bride Who Loved Country Music

The first book I ever wrote that grew my DJ business was "The Ultimate Wedding Reception," a book aimed at brides and couples planning their weddings. I intended to demonstrate my expertise and personality, so readers would feel a connection and want to hire me. One of the ways I did this was by telling stories about excellent wedding receptions, the songs that were played, and how to avoid certain mistakes with music.

I told the story about the "country line dance that went offline." The gist of the story was the bride was such a big country music fan that she wanted me to play only country music. In our consultation, I asked, "Are your friends and family attending? Are all of them country music fans?" She replied, "I don't care; it's my wedding!" I smiled and told her, "I will do my best to give you what you want. But, what's Plan B in case it doesn't work the way you think?" We agreed that I would take requests and play them by ear.

Then I told the story of what happened when we played all country line dance music, and crowds gathered around the DJ booth asking when we would play something else. I told the group that I would check with the bride. The bride got so tired of guests bugging her about other song selections she finally came to me and said, "Mark, do what you do best." I promised her we would keep the country music theme throughout the evening but only in the right places. We would also mix in a variety of hits that everybody would enjoy. The reception turned out to be a smashing success.

Demonstrating Empathy Goes a Long Way to Building Affinity

A simple story like that demonstrates empathy towards the bride and willingness to aim to please but simultaneously being ready to do whatever it takes to ensure the event is a success. If you aren't aware, in the DJ industry, many very egotistical entertainers insist it's their way or the highway. That wasn't my style. I wanted to take couples' ideas and dreams and mix them with my experience in music programming so that their celebration was both unique to them as a couple and unforgettable and fun for their guests. That's the message I focus on throughout the book.

By including stories of your experiences, perhaps with clients or in your own business, you can demonstrate the type of work that you do for your clients. At the end of the day, they want to know that you are familiar with their kind of problem and you understand entirely. I refer to this in sales because if you can explain someone's problem better than they can, you'll have them hooked.

Trust Trigger #2: The Provider

What potential clients want to know about the provider — namely, you — is how qualified you are to help them. This is closely linked to affinity. They want to know that not only do you understand their problem but that you have done what it takes to solve their problem. Do you have the criteria, certifications, or qualifications to help them overcome their problems or solve their challenges? Are you qualified to help them?

To satisfy this trust trigger, you can share stories and case studies of similar clients. Pick out some of the most common problems you know most of your prospects face. Next, reveal a unique way you helped a client overcome those challenges. If you can tell one or two of these stories, it will plant the seed that you are qualified to help. Perhaps there's a certification you earned. Maybe there is a specialized program that you created precisely for those types of problems. Tell those stories.

Trust Trigger #3: The Method

Of all the ways your prospective customers could potentially solve their problems or challenges, will your specific method work for them? The best way to communicate your method is to, once again, use stories. Maybe you can mention all the options available to solve their particular problem. You give them the pros and cons of each, and you build the case that your method is the absolute best option.

They may have tried other methods before, and perhaps they didn't get a result. It's not their fault.

It would be best if you tiptoed lightly here. Don't appear as though you're blaming your prospective customers for options that didn't work out. Instead, blame their methods but let them off the hook by reiterating it's not their fault. Explain why it's not their fault and why the methods they tried did not work as well as the option you're proposing in your book.

It Has to Seem Simple to Implement

There's another part to this trust trigger of "The Method." Not only do you have to get the reader to feel like the option you are proposing in the book is the best option, but they also have to believe that they can apply it. This means they have to believe that they can do it as well.

For example, we see this in the weight loss industry because people want the next trending method to work for them. But if they don't believe they can stick to a particular diet, getting them to sign up for your program or buy your product would be difficult.

Case Study: The Hassle of DIY

I'll give another example I use in my "Ultimate Wedding Reception" book. When I wrote the book, there was a rise in people trying to DJ their weddings using an iPod. The iPod had just come out, and with people having so many songs in their pocket, it just seemed natural that they would be able to provide music and save themselves money. Rather than blatantly saying, "You would be a fool," I chose the route of explaining precisely what was involved in DJing their own wedding if they wanted to. I let them decide. I didn't call them names. I was just spelling it all out.

After I explained the amount of equipment needed and the dozens of potential disasters that could occur, that chapter on DJing your own wedding dissuaded people from doing that very thing. It then positioned them to hire a professional DJ instead.

This is the same tactic used by astute real estate agents offering "How to - For Sale By Owner" books. They appeal to many peoples' DIY aspirations, knowing that a high percentage will give up, especially after highlighting the mountains of work it takes to list, show, and sell a home on your own. When the reader gives up, the author/agent will be the first person they call. If the agent is extra sharp, they will proactively check in on the reader's progress through automation. Readers learn to see their realtor's commission as well deserved instead of an unnecessary expense.

This delicate subject must be tested to determine the best approach for your situation. You may not want to use the appeal of "overwhelm" to gain a client. Test everything.

Case Study: Creating My Custom Motorcycle

Although I don't think it was intentional, this little technique also worked on me. In the early 2000s, I was hooked on the TV series "American Chopper" like most of the Nation, and I wanted to build a custom motorcycle. I bought books on how to make one like they were doing in the American Chopper garage. I even invested in a thousand-dollar video course where they took a group of people and built a chopper over the course of a weekend. I thought for sure I could do it with that kind of detail.

After reading the books, watching the videos, and taking the course I had invested in, I did not spend one dime on any tool. I immediately called a custom chopper shop and commissioned my bike. There was no way in Hell I would risk screwing up such a significant investment by trying to do it myself.

Trust Trigger #4: The Value Proposition

What your book's readers want to know is simple: Is your expertise and what you're proposing of great value to them? If your reader expressed interest in the form of purchasing your book or at least cracking it open if they received it for free, they are giving you something more valuable than just their money; they're giving you their time. They want to know answers, so the great benefit is having a long-form composition to express value. You have a captive audience. You can now show the value comparison of what you do against all other options available to the reader, including doing nothing at all.

In fact, you can express what it could cost them by not taking action. Value is also determined partly by the cost or risk of not taking action or implementing what you propose. As mentioned in other areas of the book, this is the salt in the recipe—just a pinch of salt; never too much salt. But the reader must be reminded of what is at stake because that is part of your value proposition.

More Cheese, Less Whiskers

It would be best if you did this very tactfully. A guru named Dean Jackson teaches a lesson called "Cheese and Whiskers." Consider this lesson when crafting your book. Jackson states that a mouse will do anything it takes, including clawing through a wall, to get to a piece of cheese. But that same mouse will scatter at even the whisper of what seems to be whiskers of a cat. With this in mind, ask yourself, "Is what I'm writing cheese, or is it whiskers?" That's the filter you need to use during the writing process to see whether your book sounds salesy or is teaching something valuable to your readers. Be mindful and tactful as you write.

Trust Trigger #5: The Status Effect

Perhaps this is the most crucial trust trigger you need to express throughout your book because people want to know how this will change their status. Will purchasing this product, working with this author, or hiring this person raise or lower their status?

There are two parts to the status effect. Potential clients will ask themselves, "When people find out I am working with this accomplished author or expert in the field, will it raise my status with family, friends, co-workers, colleagues, the business community, or within my company? On the other hand, will it lower my status?"

The second part of the status effect involves what happens if the solution fails. "What if I hire this person and it is a mess? Will it bring shame and drop my status? How will that impact how my family, friends, colleagues, and business associates see me?"

It will help if you can share stories to allay people's fears and make them feel comfortable in any way, shape, or form. You can use stories that express what it will be like working with you and how it will transform them, their business, or their lives, depending on what you do. Think of many ways to say that it's safe to work with you and that there is almost no reason for failure. Alternatively, is there a failsafe in case something doesn't work quite exactly right the first time? Quelling people's fears will bring them closer to you and the sale. The purpose of your book is to get people comfortable about working with you and hiring you. Perhaps the next step is a face-to-face appointment; your book is a predecessor to that engagement.

By its mere existence, your book inherently solves many of the possible status issues I raised above. If your reader needs to share this information with a partner, a colleague, or a spouse, rather than sharing sales material such as brochures, they can hand over your book. How much better is that? Again, people already view your book with respect. Now your prospective client can share this book and let people know that you are the person they are choosing to work with.

On the other side of the coin, let's talk about what not to include.

Be Careful Not to Appear Salesy

First, you don't want to give too many teases without giving out actual information. For example, with lines such as, "In my course, I give students X, Y, and Z," people assume the information is in your book, so give them the information.

Next, don't include too many blatant testimonials. I made this newbie mistake when I treated my book as a sales letter. In a sales letter, where people already know and expect it to sell something, you can blanket your sales piece with testimonials, case studies, and clients' results because you're trying to give them an overwhelming preponderance of proof. You can't do that in your book. Your book should look like an educational resource, not a NASCAR stock car decked out in ads.

It also helps if you don't talk too much about yourself before discussing the reader and their problems. This is another rookie mistake a lot of people make not only in books but also in advertising. Many people think they need to talk about the company's history, why they started it, how long they've been in business, and how their great-grandfather founded the company. But the reality is, as Theodore Roosevelt famously said, "People don't care how much you know until they know how much you care."

Finally, make sure that you do not include too much promotion of other products or services for sale. You can tactfully mention, in passing perhaps, a program that you have when you're telling a story of a client and their results. But never say, "If you want to join this program, go here." Sprinkle any promotion of products or services for sale very lightly. One call to action at the end of the book is usually enough.

We'll talk about other engagement devices later in the book because you will want to entice interactivity in the right places, not necessarily for paid promotions, but perhaps for free downloads, checklists, or other valuable resources related to your topic.

Remember the five trust triggers above and try to come up with a list of stories and examples you can talk about throughout your book.

KEY TAKEAWAYS

- Make sure your book has a DNA statement.
- Your book can do the heavy lifting of establishing your credibility and authority, so when it comes to customer consultations, much of the "selling" has already taken place ahead of time.
- Use all five trust triggers to maximize your book's impact on your target audience and get them to view you as a trusted advisor instead of a salesperson.
- Don't confuse your book with a sales letter.
- Always seek to inform and advise your readers instead of trying to sell them.
- Stories go a long way in demonstrating your authority and expertise instead of mere claims.

CHAPTER THREE

Show Me the Money: Using Your Book as the Nucleus of Your Business

"Books live the longest, they live beyond you, and last. They are your legacy."
— *Russell Brunson*

A common preconceived notion works to your benefit: People think that authors write books to make money by selling books. Accordingly, most of your competitors instantly discard the thought of writing books to promote their businesses. They think along the lines of, "I'm not in the bookselling business. I'm an attorney, a financial advisor, or (insert any profession here)."

This is why the idea of authoring a book never crosses their minds, which is also excellent news for you! Let them continue to think that; it ultimately equals less competition in your field.

Why write a book to promote your business? Becoming an author instantly catapults your status above your competitors. This is truly the leapfrog theory at work!

From Dime a Dozen Seller to Unique Expert

Your book can form the nucleus of your business since you can leverage the title "author" to gain an advantage over your competitors, leaving them to fight tooth and nail for the scraps. That's right; the moment you become a published author, you are perceived as an authority in your industry. Books are not merely part of a more extensive marketing tactic. Instead, book publishing is an entire transformational strategy and marketing tool.

Business legend Jay Abraham teaches a concept called "The Strategy of Preeminence," where he defines a client as someone under the care, protection, and wellbeing of another. You want to be viewed as that trustworthy advisor. Being seen as an educator and advocate in your industry is a concept far separated from a salesperson. Preeminence is about transforming and defining who you are; nothing will accomplish that better than a book.

Take it from me; I've explored all types of marketing channels, from radio to television to even DVD movie formats. Although these are also helpful, they take a backseat to having your own book. Should you try those other channels? Sure, if you have the luxury of time and resources. But, I must emphasize, do them only after you publish your book.

Books are so highly regarded that CEOs and high-level executives at Fortune 500 companies are almost expected to have books. Indeed, many top executives and CEOs at major corporations are published authors. Their books act to both reinforce and grow their industry authority and position. Their books bring home the point that they are at the top of their field.

Can you think of a more potent source of job security than being known as a book author on your subject? Don't you think your employer would be proud of that fact? Don't you think your company would consider you an indispensable asset because you're an industry authority?

Since so few of your competitors bother to write a book detailing their expertise, becoming a published author will quickly catapult you to the top tier of your industry.

Your Author Status Will Attract Other Influential Authorities in Your Field

When I attend events and am on the panel with other speakers who are also book authors, it is almost as though we have a secret handshake. It feels like we're members of some exclusive club. Your book will say a lot about you without even saying a word. It tells the world that you're ambitious, knowledgeable, and, perhaps, even fearless because you're boldly sharing your perspectives on a subject. Now that you're in that secret society, you'll gain faster acceptance for any ideas you propose to others in your field. You'll get your phone calls returned. You'll get invitations to join the big dogs in the tall grass. Why? Because other influencers will spot you, they will see you have a book that is a platform and that you can reciprocate.

Who Is This Book For?

This book isn't for you if you're trying to be the next Stephen King or J.K. Rowling of Harry Potter fame. Instead, I will show you how to make a ton of money even if you give your book away for free and never sell a single copy. Typical royalties in book publishing deals are about 10 to 15% and can amount to a dollar and some change per book sold. Even if you make five or six dollars per book, why care about such tiny transactions?

Remember this: the money you'll make won't come from selling your book. Your income will generate from being sought out and hired for thousands of dollars to work with you for the services you have to offer, all thanks to your book!

This isn't about authoring a book you can sell, but rather about **authoring a book that sells YOU.**

Make Millions With Your Book

Since your book simulates you delivering personal consultation, it allows you to "speak" to unlimited people without taking your time. Depending on your business, for example, if a client is worth $10,000, you only need to attract 100 clients to reach one million dollars. If a client is worth $5,000, you only need 200. Start with your income goal, and you can test how many books you need to send out to get one client. In my DJ business, every five books I send brings me one client on average. Considering it only takes $5 to ship a book, it costs me $25 to attain a client worth $2,000 or more. That makes it very easy to see that my #1 goal is to get more and more brides to request my book, and I will happily ship it for free.

If a reader can purchase your services or hire you and pay you thousands of dollars because of your book, would it make sense to obsess about the small pocket change you can make selling copies of it? Of course not.

Make Your Book Your Marketing Centerpiece

If you make your book the nucleus of your business (and all its communications and marketing efforts), your book becomes your PPP (Prime Positioning Portfolio) and number one marketing asset. In the following few chapters, I will highlight why you must use your book as your centerpiece and a positioning tool for your business. It is your ultimate business card, your organic presence, and it will replace brochures.

Thinking back, I have spent two to three dollars per copy to print an empty folder in which I placed sales pieces to give to clients.

I could have provided a book long ago for the same investment, and that book would have been perceived as carrying a higher value than an empty folder with sales pages.

Your book will define you without looking like you're trying too hard. To illustrate, let me share a little story from my DJ business.

As a hobby, I coach boxing and kickboxing. One night at the gym, when I was teaching a kickboxing class, one of my regular members enjoyed my class so much that a conversation came up. She asked me what else I did besides coaching at the gym. Most members assumed that's what I did full-time.

This woman was the founder of a relatively large mortgage company in the area, and she simply liked how I ran my class. Rather than having a lengthy conversation about what I did, I handed her a copy of my book, which happened to be "The Ultimate Wedding Reception." I merely told her that I help people with their milestone events and celebrations, and I politely excused myself to the locker room.

The next day, I received a phone call from her, and she asked me if she could hire me to be the DJ for her company's Christmas party. It was a large, elegant affair held at the Navy Pier Crystal Gardens, a very upscale venue in Chicago. At this point, I asked myself why I titled my book "The Ultimate Wedding Reception" when I could have made it more general. Still, the book did its job, and I often consider writing different versions to cover specific types of celebrations.

She wanted to set an appointment to discuss the details of her upcoming event where I would be seen as a trustworthy advisor prescribing a solution instead of selling her one.

In the following chapters, you will learn how to use your book to do the following:

- Attract cold prospects and build an audience list.
- Support your personal sales efforts.
- Draw the attention of media, reporters, radio, and television.

- Get speaking engagements.

Books are magnificent tools for growing your business because you can achieve many things simultaneously.

Books Are the Ultimate Repurposable Content Tool!

Not only can you use your book as the nucleus and playbook for your twelve-month marketing content calendar, but its content also creates the core of any other media channels or platforms you use to promote your brand. Repurpose your book's content for your podcast, blog, or YouTube channel. Your book can open doors to limitless opportunities, so I hope you're excited. Let's explore all the methods for using your book as the nucleus of your business.

KEY TAKEAWAYS

- Having a book instantly positions you as an authority in your field because most of your competitors aren't published authors.
- You earn more from service contracts/sales deals than your book's unit sales.
- Your author status will encourage other leaders and influencers in your industry to seek you out for possible collaborations or speaking opportunities.
- Instead of pressuring potential customers to buy using hard sales tactics, your book can bag you more sales by selling your expertise and industry authority.
- Your book's content can be repurposed to help you generate leads or market on social media and other platforms.

CHAPTER FOUR

Your Book as the Ultimate Lead Generator

*"The prime directive of a mouse is to
get cheese and avoid cat."*
- Dean Jackson

Most business owners promote their businesses the hard way. Their ads scream, "Buy me!" "Hire me!" "We have low rates!" "Give us a call!" The colossal error in this thinking is that these ad types appeal only to the three percent who are already in the market "to purchase in your category." So much money is wasted because if only three percent are ready to buy, and with so many choices and competition, very few will call you.

The Buying Cycle

According to the late business luminary Chet Holmes, when he presented the buying cycle percentages, "Three percent of the market is in active buying mode at any time." That means they are already looking to purchase something in your category, whatever it might be. If you're in the automotive industry and sell cars, three percent of the market is looking to purchase a vehicle this week. Seven percent are open to buying or have begun the buying process. This might mean they're researching, gathering information, and are in the process of buying in your category.

For instance, if they want to get carpets cleaned, they've already decided to get their carpets cleaned, and they're looking for choices. The next thirty percent are aware of your type of business, solution, or service, but they're not ready to purchase yet. They might consider you in the future. Another thirty percent are unaware of your solution but would be open to buying if they had more information. These are people who need a problem solved. They're not quite sure what their options are, and although yours is one of the options to solve their problems, they're unaware of the solution you can provide and need more information. Then there's another thirty percent who will never buy from you. Simply put, they are not your target market. For example, you sell steaks, and these individuals are vegetarians.

What do the buying cycles mean for your business? Ads that say, "Looking for a mortgage? Rates are really low. Give us a call," appeal only to three percent who are in the market to shop for mortgages right now. If you're a real estate agent, you might say, "Thinking of selling your home? Call me today!" Again, this ad appeals only to three percent of the market who've already decided they're selling their home and need a realtor. The problem? Your ad isn't alone. At any one time, there will be dozens of ads saying the same thing, "Call me!" Who will they call? We'll discuss answers to this question in this chapter.

Books, Not Ads, Appeal to More People

Your book can appeal to seventy percent of your market. This includes the three percent who are in buying mode now and the seven percent who are open or have begun the buying cycle and are collecting information. Then there are the thirty percent who are aware but are only considering buying in the future, and another thirty percent who are unaware of your solution but are open to buying if given more information.

How does your book appeal to all these people? Your book offers a non-threatening first contact! They can request your book safely and not fear having a hardcore sales conversation with somebody trying to pry open their wallet and extract cash. Using your book, prospective customers can collect the information they seek to make an informed decision.

For example, let's say you're a real estate agent and want more clients. Instead of saying, "Hey, you want to sell your house? Give me a call so I can pressure you into listing with me," you can promote your book titled, "The Top Dollar Home Seller's Checklist." Can you see how that will capture people who are in active mode to sell their homes immediately?

The book will also appeal to the seven percent who've just begun gathering information because this gives them the information they're looking for. It opens the door to the thirty percent of prospects who are aware of your solution but want to decide in the future. The book is something they can collect and read at their own pace. When they're ready, they'll have the book handy.

The book also reaches the other thirty percent who are unaware but open to your concepts. You've attracted them with a compelling title that appeals to one of the challenges already on their mind. Wouldn't you like that?

The concept of lead generation is to promote your book instead of your business. Your business still gets to ride along and deliver a higher perceived value because you're providing an informative book that is not seen as a sales pitch.

How to Use Your Book to Generate Leads

Here are the four steps to generating leads with your book.

Step #1: Bait Your Hook With a Great Title

Titles can communicate fundamental human needs, from escaping pain to gaining pleasure. We'll explore more of this in the later chapter on creating your book.

For now, I'd like you to get the general idea that you have to test titles and appeals because you may be surprised at what you find. Even marketing experts discover that sometimes their first instincts are not always the winning appeals. I'll give an example in my own business early on when I started learning direct response marketing. You learn lots of lessons from marketing masters, and they will tell you that people will pay more to escape pain versus gain pleasure. That was the principle. This is why prescription drug companies tend to have more significant revenues than vitamin companies.

I tested this principle early on in my DJ business. I came up with what I thought was an escaping pain title, "Ten Mistakes That Ruin Weddings and How to Avoid Them." That title got fewer responses than I expected. I discovered a distinct difference between escaping pain people already have and avoiding potential pain. Avoiding potential pain falls within a concept called prevention. It turns out prevention is a much harder sell than a cure. Just ask the guys selling fire alarms, smoke detectors, and insurance. Instead, I used the same information but changed the book's title to "How to Make Your Wedding Unforgettable and Fun." Sure, I massaged the content in the middle and turned the ten mistakes into ten positives. What I found was that infinitely more people requested the book.

What I learned from that little experiment was people generally seek aspirational appeals. I discovered that in the wedding industry, people are looking for their day to be joyful, and I surmise that people don't even want to consider that something could ruin their wedding or have a negative effect on their special day. Since then, I've always gone, whenever possible, towards an aspirational appeal. I learned this simply by rolling out and testing on a small scale. I initially promoted the first title by splitting a 1,500-bride mailing list I received. At first, I only mailed half of them. I sent 750 postcard offers for the book with the negative title. I mailed the other half of the list with the positive title the following month. If you want to call that scientific, that's a real test. I went on to create other attractive book titles such as "What Every Young Bride Needs to Know About Wedding Music," "The Ultimate Wedding Reception," and "Remarkable Receptions."

Raise Your Hand If You Want This!

Your book titles will get a proverbial hand-raise out of a crowd telling you, "Me! I'm thinking about that." If you have a list of people you think might be interested in your business but are not quite sure who to sell to or when to sell, you can quickly find out who is who. How? Those readiest to buy or most interested will request your book. For example, if you offer a free copy of "The Top Dollar Home Seller's Checklist" to an affluent neighborhood mailing list, you can quickly identify who you should sell to based on who requests your book.

Why is this so powerful? When you capture this information, you build a list. Your list decreases your dependency on advertising because you're not only capturing the small three percent who are in the market to purchase your category now, but you are also exposing your business to the other sixty-seven percent of your audience. With interested prospects on your list, even if you don't run your ad the following month, you can still reach prospective buyers with low-cost or free methods like direct mail or email. If done correctly, you should still run your ad to capture more people the following month. The bigger your list, the more prospects you can convert to appointments or sales.

Most traditional advertising channels do a terrible job of this. They don't build lists. They rely on showing their offer on paper for the random people who happen to cross that page that month. When you create a list, folks don't need to see your ad for them to regularly hear from you because you can reach them in their email or elsewhere.

Step #2: Catch Fish

The only mechanism you need to build your list is a simple web page to capture names and emails if you promise a free digital version of the book. But if you want to test and get fancier, you can offer to send them the book in the mail, which is my preference. I prefer a page that captures their complete contact information and mailing address. I will date myself, but this is similar to the mechanism we used, which was a fax form. We would have people fax us their requests, or they would call a toll-free recorded number, and I would have them leave their information after the tone.

As a colleague of mine, Johnny Campbell would say, "Put them in the box!" Capture that name, email, and contact list and build your list to nurture.

Step #3: Deliver Your Promise and Nurture the Relationship

Now that you've captured their information, whether through email, a contact, or a physical mailing list, send them what you promised. Deliver your eBook through a download link or deliver the book by mail. Once you have your prospects' contact information, you can create and choreograph a communication sequence. This series of contacts, "dripped" over time, encourages your list members and nurtures their relationship with your brand. Your programmed communications positively push them towards an eventual appointment and sale.

Artificial Insemination of a Relationship

The beauty of building a list is developing an audience and your ability to create immersion. You bring people closer to you by generating follow-up sequences with video, audio, or even text, delivering more juicy tips and answers to additional questions you frequently get. Even more compelling is when you answer questions they should ask but don't know enough to think about asking. Your book answers your prospect's questions before they decide to buy.

Express Your Personality and Values

Remember, people do business with people, so you don't want to write a school textbook or anything that sounds like one. Include your personal stories, talk about your discoveries, and admit struggles that caused you to learn things and answer people's problems. Make it personal. Your personal approach establishes your authority and expertise and adds more inspirational encouragement to meet with you or buy.

Books allow clear explanations of lengthy or complex topics, whether you sell to consumers or business to business. They help shorten your sales cycle by creating an informed consumer. An informed consumer makes for your best customer or client. They're thankful for the information, and you can even train them in how to work with you best, so they make accommodating and cooperative clients and customers.

Here's a big tip: In regulated fields like financial advisors, where there are ad restrictions, there are few restrictions on books. Books are covered more widely by our freedom of speech. You can see this evidence by looking at financial advisors promoting books on worry-free retirement and other bucket list retirement aspirational titles.

If you can think of the right angle, you can attract and build an audience list with other topics that may not be directly related to your business but are related to issues your ideal audience is passionate about.

Step #4: Expand Your Lead Generation

The following two methods have their own chapters. We'll go into details later, but I've included them here since they involve lead generation.

Repurpose

The beauty of publishing your book is that it can form the basis for other content you can use for lead generation. These can be articles, videos, and blog posts that contain calls to action that drive people to the simple lead capture page offering your book. If your book features "10 Step System to X," you can break each way into one article, and the call to action can be as simple as, "Want the other nine? Go to this website and get the whole book."

To be successful in any business, you must be consistently visible to your target audience. The best way to do it is with helpful, practical, and welcome content. Your book will be the basis of all this other content so repurpose your book.

Referrals

There's no more extraordinary tool for referrals than a book. Books can be gifted to people and loaned to friends. Remember that a book can start a relationship with somebody without you having to be there. Inside your book, if you include offers for people to download checklists or other helpful tools or information, then people who were gifted or loaned your book can get on your list. See the later chapter on referrals and referral partners for a great strategy in getting other people to enthusiastically co-promote you.

Here are a few examples of lead generation in different businesses:

Bobby Stocks is a guru who teaches entrepreneurs how to create leverageable income streams by selling online courses. He authored the book "The Business Code" so he could make a low-risk, low-investment offer to build a list of entrepreneurs who are interested in creating more leverageable income with online courses. He offers the book in many ways, sometimes "free plus shipping," where the fee actually covers the print, postage, and ad cost, making it a self-liquidating offer. With this tool, he can run his ads perpetually because they pay for themselves.

Cory Long teaches faith-based entrepreneurs how to build side hustles that create income not tied to trading time for dollars so they can spend more time in their ministry work. His book, "Digital Storefronts," is the blueprint he teaches. Cory describes the system, and the folks requesting a copy of his book identify themselves as his ideal students. Readers gain clarity and are lathered up to learn from his higher-access, higher-immersion, higher-fee coaching programs. The book defines who Cory is, who he helps, his system, and how it helps people.

Here's an exercise for you in lead generation:

Define who it is that you want to attract. What is their most burning desire? What are their everyday worries? You can search forums and Facebook groups if you want to find this information and don't know it already. Learn the pillow talk or dinner table conversations.

The great copywriter, Robert Collier, taught in his book the concept of entering the conversation already in your prospect's mind. Do this research and make these lists to get inspiration for book titles, chapter topics, and advertising appeals.

Want to learn more about in-depth lead generation? You can discover an entire cashflow-driven marketing system that builds your business or personal brand for free in my book titled "Action Brand Marketing."

KEY TAKEAWAYS

- Your book helps you build an audience who voluntarily sign up to stay in touch with you via email or physical mail.
- Your mailing list helps you efficiently walk your prospects through the sales cycle. They go from self-selected audience members to leads to sales and appointments for your business.
- Create a practical, free book your audience members can recommend, loan, or give away to others who need the answers your book provides.
- Repurpose your book to create lead magnets and other pieces of content you can use to help build your list.

CHAPTER FIVE

Your Book Boosts Your Sales

"It's beneficial not to be thought of as a salesman, and your book can be the golden master key to alternative, advantageous positioning."
— Dan Kennedy

Your book automatically transforms you from a mere salesperson to an advocate and educator to an expert and authority. If you do personal selling that requires one-on-one meetings in person, online, or by phone, there are several tactics that you can use in different situations. For those who are already uncomfortable about making sales calls or perhaps don't really like the whole sales process, this book is your ace in the hole. Your book is about sharing knowledge and education and won't be seen by your readers as being salesy. If you're looking for a sleaze-free selling method, write your book!

You won't be seen as advocating or selling your products or services when done right. Instead, your book appears as the solution to your readers' problems. The fact that you have a product or a solution for them is implied but not directly sold. If you do cold outreach to set appointments rather than leaving a business card, you can leave your book along with a note. You can precede any sales meeting with your book.

One commonly overlooked opportunity amongst salespeople is to set an appointment and do nothing until the meeting. You have so many opportunities to pre-sell your prospect before your meeting. Try sending them a copy of your book instead. I used to do this with a FedEx package and give my prospects enough time to read the book before our meeting. In fact, the letter that I included with the book instructed them to do so. Doing this creates intentional redundancy because I will go over all of those items again in person. But if they have read about it first, it gives them a grounding on the concepts we'll cover in the meeting. Because a book is long-form, it allows people to softly get to know you and immerse themselves in your expertise and brand.

By the time they meet you, you're also perceived as somewhat of a celebrity! A great thing about a book is that it enables you to immerse your audience because it is long-form content. This means you have the space and time to give them the information they require to buy from you. This is especially helpful in cases where you are selling something that is slightly complicated or requires extensive explanation.

When you lead with your book, you cut a lot of time out of the typical sales cycle because prospects can be educated in the time leading up to your face-to-face meeting.

Deliver Your Perfect Pitch Every Time

Your book lets you clone your message and deliver the perfect pitch every time. For example, you could send what I call a "wow package" in advance via FedEx. You can include printouts of news articles you have appeared in and related third-party news supporting the special or unique way your business solves customers' problems. You could include a video and, of course, a copy of your book. If you haven't set a sales appointment yet and just got an inquiry or a request for information, perhaps you can offer them that "wow package" as a free offer for direct response.

When you deliver the package of your book and cover letter, you can use your book to offer your consultation. Tell prospects to check out the book, write down any questions, and book a meeting with you. Give them your calendar link.

Before I learned this method, I was just doing the typical sending of a brochure that I printed, and these brochures would typically cost $3 to $4 each. Worse, just by the mere fact that I'm sending a brochure, I was already handicapped because people view brochures as sales materials instead of education.

I completely leveled up my results when I learned that I could deliver an educational book for less than the cost of a printed brochure. It was a no-brainer.

Use Your Book to Increase Your Show-up Rate to Appointments

One great way to ensure your prospect will actually show up for your appointment is to let them know they'll get a free copy of your book when they arrive. This also allows you to create an air of celebrity authorship when you sign the book's inside cover right before you give it to them.

Here's an Example: Marketing Strategy From Sending Your Book to Appointment

Step #1: Offer Your Book for Free or Just for Covering the Shipping Cost

You can do this through advertisements. You can offer your book as a gift when you speak on stage in front of groups and offer your book free when you do radio, TV, or podcast interviews.

Step #2: Send Your Book With a Cover Letter to People That Request It

In your cover letter, make a soft offer to answer any questions they might have.

Step #3: Follow Up and See if Your Prospect Received Your Book

After a few days, you can have your secretary or an assistant follow up and call that prospect by phone. Say something like, "This is just a courtesy call. Mark wanted to know if you've received his book and wanted me to check if you had any questions."

Step #4: Check Again if They Would Like to Have an Appointment

A few days after your first call, have your assistant call again and say, "This is a courtesy call from the office of (insert your name here) and (your name) would like to invite you for a personalized call to see how you can apply any of the strategies they shared in the book to *your* specific circumstances. Is Tuesday a good day for you?"

Show Your Authority and Exclusivity

Having a signature book helps you deliberately design your consultation environment to suggest what you want people to know about you subliminally. You want them to know that you are an author, maybe a best-selling author. You want to display your distinction, so if you have any awards, create a book display somewhere in your conference room or on your desk. If you do video meetings, stage your awards behind you in plain sight.

You want to demonstrate that you're in demand and popular. Maybe you want to show that you are well-read and well compensated. If so, fill your environment with items that reinforce this perception, like awards, framed articles that you have had in trade publications, or pictures of you meeting with industry leaders.

During your consultation, a subtle tactic is to use the book to discuss concepts. If you have a copy of your book and share a method or a tactic with them in the consultation, you could have dog-eared pages with case studies or examples to deepen the conversation.

The interesting part about this subtle tactic is that not only are you quoting from a book, like a pastor would quote scripture, but you're quoting from your own book. As I've mentioned, sign a copy of the book for them, which is a humble demonstration that "this is normal for you." You do this all the time. It's a subtle suggestion that authors do this, not salespeople.

At the end of that consultation, only a salesperson would *sell* something. An expert or an authoritative author *prescribes* something, just like a doctor determining the symptoms of the problems and then prescribing the solution. You want to be seen as giving a prescription that is a solution to their pain instead of an offer to buy what you're selling.

One more thing you can do in your sales appointment or consultation is to stimulate referrals. When all is said and done, whether or not you have signed them as a new client, you can encourage referrals by simply supplying your client or prospect with more copies of your book to give to family, friends, and colleagues. Ask them how many they could use. Tell them just to ask if they need more.

They will feel proud to tell the story about hiring the author of (insert the title of your book here), and now you, in their mind, are a business celebrity, not a salesperson. That little subtle extra pride in hiring the best kicks in, and that could help them share your books with their family, friends, and colleagues.

Your book is the greatest asset you could use to catapult your personal sales. Use it humbly but use it. Leverage your book during your sales cycle and before and after your sales appointment.

Key Takeaways

- Use your book to boost your credibility before a sales meeting or free consultation.
- Your book does the heavy work of introducing you and establishing your authority and expertise.
- Recap key parts of your book when addressing your prospect's problems during meetings or online consultations.
- Subtly show off authority-boosting items in the room you're meeting your prospect in.
- Your book enables you to come off as an expert prescribing solutions instead of a salesperson trying to close a deal.

CHAPTER SIX

Using Your Book to Attract Media

*"A good PR story is infinitely more
effective than a front-page ad."*
— Sir Richard Branson

T here's a long-running theory in marketing that brands are not launched by advertising but by publicity. Advertising merely maintains what publicity builds. In the case of small businesses and professionals in private practice, nothing gets your name out there with more credibility than the endorsement of a trusted third-party platform, and that is what getting media attention is all about.

Let's discuss the how, what, and why of using your book to attract as much media attention as you want.

The Real Power of Radio, TV, or Podcast Interviews

Imagine appearing on Fox or ABC and being presented as a guest expert on your topic. The popular host introduces you as the author, or if appropriate, the best-selling author of "INSERT THE TITLE

OF YOUR BOOK HERE." The host shares a few tidbits with the audience, including your credentials, significant achievements, or awards you've won. Your appearance allows you to demonstrate your depth of knowledge, affinity, and personality. Can you see how being endorsed by a trustworthy authority or news channel catapults your status more than any front-page advertisement?

What is more important than appearing in a broadcast is what you do with the recording of your appearance. Leverage the recording in your marketing. I've seen too many professionals that don't do this. They think of the appearance as a one-time organic act; whatever comes of it is all they get. But they need to understand that they can use it for many years by obtaining the recording of the television broadcast or radio broadcast and using it as a marketing tool. You can use the video as an ad or edit it, so you have multiple clips to use for social posts. Add your call to action at the end to maximize efficacy. If you were on the show talking about content from your book, a natural offer would be for folks to get a copy of your book or an excerpt from it, even if you give it away for free to build your mailing list.

Use Your Book as Bait

Whether on TV, radio, or podcasts, hosts only want guests who will make them look good. They want guests who will deliver what their audience wants. Hosts care more about their audience's happiness than they do about you. You can become a media darling when you start to gain a reputation for delighting and engaging audiences. Once your reputation precedes you, you will have show hosts coming to you.

Have you ever noticed that the majority of guest experts who appear on shows happen to be book authors? This is no accident. Hosts choose authors first because the mere fact that they are an author shows that the program's host has a bonafide expert on the show. It is a shortcut for everyone. It is an anchor. Like everyone else, people are looking for shortcuts to understanding who you are, what you're about, and what value you bring if they do not know you yet. The TV show host wants to telegraph who you are and what you're about, and nothing does it more straightforward than the title of your book.

The mere fact that you're an author subliminally tells the audience that they are in the right place to acquire some qualified knowledge from a real expert. Rather than just send a press release to these media outlets, include a copy of your book with a cover letter sharing the topics and angles you can discuss. Ideally, those topics are currently in the news, and you can tie your information to them. While your book might age in theory, in reality, you can angle it to whatever is current in the news at the time. Ideally, a lot of your book's content should be evergreen. The media wants stories and ideas to talk about. They can view your book as a collection of content they are looking for.

In short, being an author makes you an expert. You make reporters look good when they are interviewing experts.

Here are some tips.

Tip #1: Consider labeling chapters according to hot topics in the news or key evergreen topics.

Tip #2: Consider the seasons of the year. What topics are hot in what parts of the year in your industry?

If you're an expert in the wedding industry, these topics include spring weddings, people getting engaged in February during Valentine's Day, or fall and winter weddings. Consider these seasons and plan a marketing calendar, or send your media kits and books to shows according to these times of the year.

Tip #3: Determine what topics in your book are controversial. Can you develop a well-documented and well-supported view that bucks against conventional wisdom about a specific topic?

Audiences love controversy, mainly if you can shed some light on a trending topic. I don't necessarily mean being contrarian by controversy, but perhaps your topic has a double-entendre or some secondary belief that is also true.

What if You Wrote a Monthly Column in Your Industry's Largest Trade Journal?

How much easier would it be to get accepted by a magazine as a columnist if you were the author of an authoritative book on the subject? The quickest way to go from invisible to the top of the food chain is by sending these trade organizations and trade magazines your book. When your book arrives on the editor's desk, you come out of nowhere and become a contender for the media outlet.

I've personally landed columns in two different industries — the mobile DJ industry and the direct response marketing industry — by using this tactic. I've written several articles for Mobile Beat Magazine and DJ Times. In marketing, I wrote the "Grow Your Local Business" column for Dan Kennedy's No BS Marketing Letter for three years. The value of being a column author is priceless, and it has led to many clients. All of the articles were based on the content in my books. Your book is not a one-and-done deal. It becomes your playbook for the life of your career. Start your business journey by writing your book.

If you're just beginning your career or business, you're lucky that you learned this first. Many people who have put this off for years and years wish they had done it first.

Want Another Insider Secret About Getting Media?

Media attracts media. Nothing shows a producer your abilities and affability better than seeing you on another show. But what if you have no other appearances?

Here's a Tip: (Drum Roll, Please)...Manufacture It!

It doesn't matter to a show producer if the show you appear on is big or small. They are looking at you and how you talk and present, and they are looking to see if you are an excellent interviewee or are coachable. They want to know that you can speak in sound-bites and don't ramble on.

For my authors, I've created a program with a TV producer that allows us to sponsor segments on several TV channels across the country and feature our authors as guests. These are bonafide TV appearances on Fox, ABC, and other established media platforms, with the appearances broadcast on their specific channels.

Most importantly, the authors get recordings they can use for years to come. The media network's logo appears on the video, whether it's Fox, ABC, or NBC. This goes a long way in lending credibility when you use video footage on social posts and advertisements. Viewers see you differently after you appear on those established, trustworthy media platforms.

Want a quick jumpstart to getting media attention? It's actually quite simple: sponsor a segment. For everything I mentioned earlier, like getting the video recording to use for advertising, it's a double whammy because even if you run paid advertising to show your video, it appears like news.

Like Sir Richard Branson said: "It is perceived as more credible and therefore more effective than any front-page ad." This is especially true for professionals in private practice and small businesses. Nothing builds credibility and authority faster than the endorsement of high-authority media channels, including known brands like ABC or Fox. Nothing gets you on those programs easier and faster than having your own book. Once you have a book under your belt, you can choose to take your business brand to a whole other level by choosing to become a media darling.

For more information on sponsored segments, go to Books-GrowBusiness.com.

KEY TAKEAWAYS

- Use your book as bait for media interviews or column writing opportunities for your industry's trade journals or top publications.
- Manufacture your media appearances by booking podcast interviews.
- Use your podcast appearances as dress rehearsals and "try-outs" for larger mainstream media platforms.
- Jumpstart your media appearances by shooting a video and paying for placement on local TV platforms.

CHAPTER SEVEN

Turning Your Book Into the Ultimate Referral Tool

"The only thing more important than the size of your network is the quality of your network."
— *Ivan Misner, BNI*

Referrals are the lifeblood of any business. Which marketing tactic do you think has the greatest return on investment? Do you think it's email marketing? Pay-per-click advertising? Most entrepreneurs are surprised to learn that referrals, also known as word of mouth, yield the best marketing ROI. Technically speaking, referrals require no advertising expenditure. Even better, they bring in highly qualified prospects.

According to Nielsen, 84% of people trust recommendations from people they know, and those people are four times more likely to make a purchase when they are referred by a friend. When an ideal customer or client refers you to a friend, peer, colleague, or family member, they are essentially bringing you new prospects who share their own qualities. These newly referred clients often turn out to be ideal customers themselves. When one client you bring in from advertising turns into two, you have cut the acquisition cost of that client or customer in half and doubled your ad campaign revenue.

Get Your Customer Base to Multiply Itself

Could you imagine if every client or customer referred you to at least one other person? What would that do for your business? Wouldn't it essentially double your business? Your book is one of the most effective referral-generating tools you can have in your arsenal, and in this chapter, you'll find out how.

To quickly get started with referral marketing, simply arm your existing clients with books they can hand out. Right after releasing your book, reach out to your complete customer base, not only recent clients and customers but also past ones. In fact, your book's launch makes for a great reason to reach out to past customers. This applies to even "lost" customers. Don't stop at asking to send them just one book. Tell them you'd love to send them multiple copies if they ask.

When one of your existing clients recommends your book to a friend or colleague, you are more likely to be seen as an educator or an advocate rather than a salesperson. Compare this to when someone refers you to others by passing along your business card. In that context, you look more like a salesperson.

In the past week alone, I've received two book recommendations from two separate people about two totally different topics. I purchased both books without even researching them because I already know and trust the colleagues who gave the referrals. Imagine if you gave a handful of books to each of your clients, and they recommend your book to a friend and hand them a signed copy. This type of recommendation links to the trust trigger of status that we discussed in the previous chapter because people will refer you much more readily if doing so raises their status at no risk to them. In this case, perhaps they get to brag that they work with you. Perhaps, they get to brag that they're so close with you that they own signed copies of your book. If these clients know, like, and trust you, and you've done everything right so they know you will serve their friends well, you could earn their referral.

When you send these books to your clients, you should always include a personal letter stating that referrals are the lifeblood of your business and you sincerely appreciate them. Always let people know what you're looking for and never leave it to chance. Create a referral culture within your business.

Let Others Give Away Your Book as "Thank You" Gifts

In your business, do you work with other vendors that are complementary service providers that you share common clients with? You could do one or two things with them to help both of you.

First, you could position your book, a helpful guide that solves potential customers' problems, as a gift that vendors can give away to their clients with a purchase or as a "thank you." For example, in my wedding DJ business, when I released my book "The Ultimate Wedding Reception," I offered it to complementary vendors, including photographers, bridal shops, videographers, and live bands. I simply gave each vendor a small box of books and the cover letter, letting them know that they could give away those books free of charge to any of their clients and customers. I also made it a point to note that the free book adds value to the services my complementary vendors provided and that they can position the book as a "thank you" gift to their customers. This allowed those vendors to give away a valuable gift of information that would help their client or customer and, at the same time, subtly promote my business.

Another approach is to make your book part of a collaborative goody bag. What I mean by that is gathering the same complementary vendors and finding a free gift that each of you can contribute. For you, it could be your book. Using the DJ example, I offered my book. The live band would contribute a CD of their music. A photographer or a videographer could include a free entry-level 'sampler' of their service or maybe a guide on choosing the right photographer or videographer. It's all about being creative and having an abundance mindset. Instead of seeing people as competition, focus on cooperation. I call it "co-opetition."

The live bands I worked with had no problem handing out my book about a DJ because people working with a live band have already decided they will work with a live band. And my DJ information was not going to talk them out of it. In fact, in my business, we already successfully incorporated DJ music with live bands, so both benefited. I've done hundreds of weddings and bar mitzvahs with a live band and DJ combination.

When you gather complementary vendors together, you get the power of cross-promotion because each vendor contributes their own new clients to the mix-increasing every cooperating vendor's marketing reach. If your goody bag or "thank you" gift bag is distributed to each of your new clients, you're effectively getting cross-promotion for free.

Books Fix the #1 Referral Failure

Often, if you have a service that requires some explanation or demonstration for people to understand, your client will twist and contort your explanation to the person they are trying to refer to you. The would-be referrer can be so confusing that their explanation could actually deter referrals from calling you.

Remember the sales principle of face-to-face selling, which is to always present with all decision-makers in the room? The reason is that you can spend an hour giving an uncomplicated presentation. Still, if that person you're meeting with can't decide without their spouse's blessing, they will simply go home and provide the worst summary of your hour-long presentation to their spouse. They'll likely get so confused that the spouse will be cross-eyed. They might say, "I don't think that sounds like a good idea."

Books solve the dilemma above once and for all. Your book will deliver your message perfectly, and all a referring client has to do is hand out a copy of your book and say, "Take a look at their method. I think you'll like it." Plus, you just subtly demonstrated to your spouse that the person you are considering working with is someone to be respected because they are a published author, which can drop their suspicion. Hence, they are more open to the conversation, to begin with.

Books allow you to can and clone your presentation so it delivers a perfect pitch every time. Books eliminate the confusion and "telephone game" of misinformation in typical verbal referrals. Plus, books trigger the sense of status and feeling of pride your clients get when they say, "My guy wrote the book on (insert field of expertise here)," right before giving your book to a referral.

Referral Partner Database Gift

This is an excellent tactic if you have a complementary referral partner. Both of you come up with offers that you can make to your own individual lists for a free gift from the other referral partner. For example, in my wedding DJ business, I would ask my videographer friend to email his entire customer client list to announce a terrific new book about creating fabulous wedding receptions. The email would offer the book free of charge if list members asked for it. Since my videographer promotions partner was sending the message to his list, his announcement of my free book offer amounts to an endorsement. I would then return the favor by making an offer about the videographer to my own client list. I would offer whatever my videographer referral partner wanted to promote this time.

Another version of this marketing method involves doing everything for your referral partner so they don't have to lift a finger. All they need to do is lend you their mailing list; you handle everything else. You take care of everything from paying postage to shipping out the book. This includes sending books and a handwritten note that positions your book as a gift from one of the vendors they already do business with. Your book enables you to leverage the trust your partner's list members already have with your partner.

Building Goodwill From Your Referral Partner

Find a way to mention a referral partner in your book. This is also a great way to get the attention of a dream referral partner you do not yet have. A simple compliment goes a long way. A mention of the value they bring as a complementary service to your reader can create reciprocity.

If you want to go beyond a simple mention, you could go as far as a short interview with that person for a chapter within your book. This is a great way to break the ice with a dream referral partner you do not yet have. Simply reach out to them and let them know that you're writing a book for an audience you share and would like to interview them for a chapter in your book. Imagine the feeling that will create!

I learned this secret when I heard about a motivational speaker in the 1970s that mentioned Amway in his book and then sent it to the founders of Amway. His praise of the company prompted Amway to send that book to their entire distributor base and prospective distributors. This one mention led to a lifelong relationship between the motivational speaker and Amway in the form of regular speaking engagements at their events. In addition to adding a lot more dollars to his bank account, such speaking gigs also exposed the motivational speaker to other money-making opportunities.

This is the powerful referral secret you need to consider. You cannot take this lightly.

Book Licensing Opportunities

This advanced technique involves letting related vendors or complementary services within your industry license your book to use in their marketing campaigns. You gain a referral partner if you offer services that can supplement what they're doing. For example, my wedding reception entertainment book is licensed all over the U.S. and Canada. I have licenses with other wedding DJ entertainers who get the privilege of putting their names on my book as co-authors and using it in marketing campaigns. Even though they know the power of marketing through books, they licensed my book because very few people know where to start regarding book writing. Many don't want to go through the trouble of writing their own book.

With book licensing, you can have folks using your book all around the country to promote their services. If you happen to offer a service they don't necessarily provide; you can offer to fulfill it for them for additional revenue. That way, you gain a referral partner. At a minimum, you gain a licensing fee. If you structure your book to maintain your name as co-author, you get a promotional partner that is paying you for the privilege of further spreading your author brand.

As you've discovered, books are powerful referral tools. They deliver your message accurately and make it easy for your clients to refer you by simply handing out your book. They're a valuable platform that will attract many referral partners as it strokes their ego so much they can't help but participate.

KEY TAKEAWAYS

- Turn your book into a referral magnet by using it to cater to the status trust trigger: People naturally want to look good to their friends and associates. By giving out your book, their name is associated with that of an industry expert.

- Set up free book distribution deals with other non-competing vendors and service providers who serve the same target audience as you. They can use your book as a value-added premium that rewards loyal customers while helping promote your services.

- Find non-competing businesses that service your target audience. Cut a deal with them where you mail out your free book to their client list in exchange for them using your book as a 'reward.'

- Look into offering your book as a licensing opportunity where others in your industry can pay you a licensing fee for the right to put their name as a co-author of your book. As an additional bonus, you get free exposure when they distribute the book in their market.

CHAPTER EIGHT

Speaking Opportunities and Ethical Trojan Horses

*"Whether persuasion or manipulation is
good or bad boils down to intent."*
— Mark Imperial

I f you offer to give a presentation to the members of an organization
or trade association, you will be met with suspicion. They'll want
to know what you're trying to sell. They'll just assume that you're
up to something.

Your book will disarm skeptics. You can lower an organization's
guard by letting them know you wrote a book that will help their
audience and offering a free workshop to their members, including
Q&A sessions. This method makes you appear non-threatening,
your content helps people, and you gain valuable exposure and access
to their membership.

The most incredible opportunity offered to professionals is the
ability to speak in front of groups. Group speaking does so much
in terms of building your authority. At the end of your speech,
you can offer one-on-one consultations to the audience and book

multiple appointments from one presentation. As you can see, speaking one-to-many is a very effective, efficient approach.

Your book can open doors that mere mortals with business cards cannot walk through. Your book can even open doors where previously you were seen as a competitor or someone not worth inviting.

There have been events in the DJ industry where organizations would see me as a typical trade association member. Having written a book on wedding receptions and a book for the industry on how to improve the marketing of a DJ entertainer business, I've been invited to speak internationally. I pretty much came out of nowhere and was speaking on associations' stages within months of advertising my book. Previously, no one in the industry, except for my local competitors, knew my name.

Many association members wished they had been invited to that stage. Many had been decades-long trade association members. Some were even well-known among their peers. Still, my book was the tool I used to get trade industry speaker spots, leapfrogging industry veterans in the process.

Send Your Book to Trade Associations and Organizations

One great way to get your foot in the door is to send your book to your target industry's trade associations. These are groups whose members are the people you serve. Include a cover letter letting them know that you've just released a new book and you're doing a book tour to get the word out. Ask them if they would like to be included in your tour calendar. In the package, have a "speaker one-sheet" so they can quickly learn about your background.

Depending on the situation and the value of their audience to you, you might want to provide free copies of your book to all attendees. As you become known, you may consider asking for speaking fees and even require a bulk book buy for their audience as part of your package. As an added value-boosting bonus, let the association know you would be willing to autograph copies personally.

What to Do if the Event Promoter Does Not Allow You to Sell From the Stage

Although there are a lot of events that sell high-ticket, multi-thousand-dollar programs from the stage, there are some organizations that simply do not allow sales. By doing so, they think they are protecting their audience and members. They're actually doing their audiences a disservice, but that's a controversial topic for a different book.

To get around this common no-selling policy, as I mentioned earlier, you may want to offer complimentary copies of your book. Alternatively, many trade organizations will make an exception if you sell your book for less than $15 or $20. Even if you offer your book at a half-price discount, you'll still profit from each book sold, give a great value to the audience, and build a customer list.

One ethical list-building tactic I've used was to tell people from the stage that if they would like a copy of my book, they could pass their business card down to the center of the aisle, and my assistant would collect it. The idea was that it was a forthcoming book, or I didn't have them on site and would ship copies to them.

Another tactic you can apply is to set up a table in the back of the room after your talk. Let people know they can bring their business cards to the table in exchange for a book. I handed my books out like water because it enabled me to offer those folks a strategy session by phone. I would sell them on a high-ticket coaching program or high-ticket recurring services during the call. The same offer was inside the book. One way or another, I had unlimited opportunities to nurture a relationship with that prospect.

Some Event Promoters Allow High-Ticket Selling From the Stage

For some promoters, selling from the stage is a significant part of their revenue. If you get approved to speak at an event that allows stage selling, you need to determine what type of program you will be selling from the stage. These can be sold for hundreds or even thousands of dollars.

If you're speaking at a stage selling event, you may not want to offer your book on an à la carte basis. You would only sabotage yourself if you did this. You'd be simultaneously offering a high-ticket item while giving your audience a low-ticket alternative in the form of your book. You would end up giving them a low-cost option to scratch their itch. At events where you are allowed to sell from the stage, make your book part of the more expensive package you offer. Bundle it with your high-ticket offer to increase your offer's perceived value.

It is typical for a promoter of these types of events to expect a revenue share of 50% of your sales from the stage. This is fair, considering you didn't spend a penny recruiting the audience, and the promoters bear all the expenses, such as renting the room. Plus, they've spent quite a bit on advertising over the years to build their audience and membership.

Create Your Own "Evening With the Author"

Many of our clients are in financial services and use dinner seminars to gain clients. I teach them to change their dinner seminars into themes called "An Evening With the Author." Once they make the switch, many of these advisors see a dramatic increase in response and attendance. These events can be promoted perpetually month in and month out using social media advertising like Facebook ads, YouTube ads, and even direct mail to the right mailing list.

There is something more fascinating about an "Evening With the Author" than a typical financial service dinner seminar where everyone knows the person in front of the room is selling something. Since so few of your competitors have published a book, you have instantly separated yourself into your own category. Being an expert published author gives you a tremendous competitive advantage. You also gain the added benefit of appearing fresh in your field.

Your book automatically differentiates you from the rest of your field. Suppose the title of your book is a hot topic, and you're offering a question-and-answer session or fireside chat over dinner. In that case, you and your audience can directly have a meaningful conversation about topics from your book. This makes for a simply more appealing and disarming format to get even skeptical people to drop their guard and want to attend.

Join Influencers and Other One-Percenters

The great part of having a book is now you're playing in the tall grass with the big dogs. You can send your book to other influencers in your field who complement rather than compete with your expertise and collaborate on fun and effective promotions. People are much more likely to return your phone calls and emails when they receive a book from a "fellow author." You can co-promote "Evening With the Author" events with these other influencers. You can do podcasts together and cross-promote speaking engagements with each other.

The bottom line? Once you've transformed yourself into a published author, you now have the keys to the castle. You have gained your seat at the head table, and the world is your oyster.

Nothing goes together more naturally than a published author and speaking engagements. There is nothing more profitable than being able to speak to large audiences, whether in person, on stage, or on a webinar endorsed by a trade organization or other list owner that already has your ideal prospects.

KEY TAKEAWAYS

- Leapfrog seasoned industry veterans who are not authors and apply for speaking opportunities at trade organizations leveraging your published author status.
- Proactively contact other local industry or related trade groups catering to your target audience to book you as a free or paid speaker.
- Give away your book for free or at a discounted rate at speaking events.
- Don't sell your book individually when allowed to sell big-ticket programs from the stage. Instead, bundle it with a big ticket offer to boost your premium offer's perceived value.
- Use your book and the industry group speaking experience to gain the attention of other industry influencers. Co-promote each other by speaking at the same events and marketing to each other's follower base.

CHAPTER NINE

Three Essential Book Formats

"One type of book shows the world who you are;
another shows them that others think you're great."
— Mark Imperial

You should have three essential types of books in your Prime Positioning Portfolio, and you will learn about all three in this chapter. Two of the types have the same perspective. The only difference between the first two types is that one type is shorter than the other. The third has a different perspective that bolsters your credibility. The first two types show how "you view the world." The third type shows how the "world views you." Let's take a look at all three.

Book Type #1 - Your Signature Book (Your Perspectives)

Why should you create this type of book? Because you will use this book as your identifier, your DNA, that's why I call it your signature book. Your signature book gives your audience a shortcut to understanding who you are and what you do, which is paramount in today's distracted, short-attention-span world.

This book helps define you, your values, and who you stand for and against. It will educate your readers to give them confidence in you because they can clearly understand what you're about. This book will also help your readers overcome their fears to reach their goals and dreams. Simply put, this book will define your brand.

When should you create your signature book? Ideally, the answer is yesterday.

Memorialize Your Method

One of the most powerful things you can do with your book is to anchor your method or system with your name in the mind of your target audience. Do you have a system or unique way of doing things? Yes, you do, even though you might not think so.

Your goal here is to identify your current system of doing things and brand it. Formalize your methods by putting down what you do and how you do it on paper. Next, give your process a sexy name. Come up with something you can consistently put in front of people, promote, and explain.

Maybe you're thinking, "Aw shucks, Mark! I went to the same school and learned my craft like everybody else, so I'm just doing the same thing everybody else does."

Well, don't you worry because that would be impossible. You may follow the standard steps that everybody learned from the same place. However, each person puts their own spin on things, and the one thing that people cannot commoditize is you. You and I and every other individual on the planet have our own collective mentors, beliefs, or schools. We've all learned different things from different places. All that variety of experiences makes us perform our craft differently. Use this fact to your advantage and give your way of doing things a name. Whether you are an attorney, a CPA, a financial advisor, or another professional service provider, you put your own spin on how you perform.

Your job at this point is to share your unique system with the world. Use your book to give your system a name.

Your Signature Book Helps You Avoid Google Commoditization

Pamela Yellen wrote "Bank on Yourself," describing her proprietary investing methods. At the end of the day, the book focused on a specific type of whole life insurance. Her book's unique way of using that whole life insurance made her stand out. However, had she mentioned whole life insurance anywhere on the book cover, the title, or telegraphed it anywhere else, it would send people straight to Google (or running for the hills).

When people type "whole life insurance" into a search engine, millions of results appear. Every prospective reader of Yellen's book would have headed straight into a rabbit hole never to be seen again, finding a whole heap of mixed and unreliable information on whole life insurance. This is Google commoditization and what you want to avoid.

Instead, when they search "Bank on Yourself Pamela Yellen," all results point to her, and her status is raised as a thought leader and creator of a unique methodology. This is why you want to memorialize your method and give it a unique name. You want prospects to find your specific way, so they can be exposed to your method and recognize you as the creator.

To overcome Google commoditization, you must de-link yourself and what you do from commoditization. Is there a term that you can create for your method that is honest and ethical? It should describe what you do, but it should not be a commoditized term that everybody thinks they know something about. You want something that has zero preconceived notions to create uniqueness and fascination.

Consider your book titles carefully. We will cover this topic in-depth in the chapter on "Easy Authorship." Still, it would be best if you kept in mind that although this is considered a signature book, the idea is not to create an "everything-you-need-to-know -from-A-to-Z" encyclopedia on the subject. Nobody has that kind of attention span today. In fact, this kind of title would be detrimental. Brevity is the key here, and you will learn more in that chapter.

Your signature book is intended to help you demonstrate your specialized knowledge. You're not keeping secrets from anyone. However, you want to give them a bird's-eye view of the process. Give them a greater understanding of how you do things and what you believe, and offer them a way to get more or to connect with you. This is how you take your reader from prospect to appointment. Signature books, of course, are written in the first person to build a rapport between you and potential future clients.

In your signature book, you can include case studies of clients you want to attract more of. The aim is that your ideal client will relate to your stories and buy your product or engage your services. Your book can also include just a handful of testimonials from those ideal cases. Only have a few testimonials, about three to five. Please don't overdo it, or your book may start to look like a sales pitch.

If your book shows the reader that you understand their problem better than they do and have the knowledge and experience to help them, you become attractive for them to hire.

Book Type #2 - Sizzle Book or "Ask-the-Expert Book" (Your Perspectives)

This short-form book type defines your identity, similar to a signature book. Why create a sizzle book or "ask-the-expert" style book? The short answer is that this type of book can be published quickly. It's pocket-sized and convenient. You can use it as the ultimate business card. It's also a great way of highlighting your field specialties in case you have multiple. You can publish a sizzle book for each of your specialties, creating a collection.

For example, in family law, perhaps you specialize in divorce cases involving families with children. Maybe your practice also focuses on working with business owners going through divorces. You can have separate sizzle books for each specialty. This works great because people would prefer to have a specialized book than one big fat book with everything under the sun in it. That type of book just won't feel special to them. Remember, people want to know that you specialize in solving their particular problems.

Sizzle books or "ask-the-expert" books are meant for one problem, one solution, and they involve deep specialization. While crafting your signature book, you can use one or more sizzle books to start getting clients immediately. It is the fastest way to get a credible book out there.

The sizzle book or "ask-the-expert" format is more popular than you think. It's an interview-style format that mimics a radio or television interview. Do you want proof of how popular this format is? Check out the hugely popular book by Gary Vaynerchuk, or "Gary Vee" as you might know him, titled "#AskGaryVee." This book was simply a compilation of his answers to the most frequently asked questions he received on his podcast. Simple to organize, easy for readers to consume.

Gary Vee's book format demonstrates a key point: you can quickly compile your existing materials to publish your sizzle book or "ask-the-expert" book. Whether you create this book from scratch or repurpose your existing content, this format ensures you can publish your book in a matter of hours, not weeks.

Book Type #3 - Anthology Book
(Third-Party Endorsement)

An anthology is a book with many contributors based around a common theme. A common thread brings together these complementary expert peers. These themed books educate the prospect on the contributors' specialized fields. This type of book demonstrates that the world recognizes you as an authority, a powerful third-party endorsement.

Here is a quick rundown of some anthology titles we published so you can get a good idea of the kind of topics found in anthologies:

- "Leading Advisor" and "Remarkable Retirement" assembled a roundtable of financial advisors and wealth managers nationwide around a central topic.
- "Real Estate Insights" brought together real estate agents from different parts of the country, sharing the state of their market after the pandemic.
- "Post-Pandemic Profits" brought together marketing experts in different categories, discussing how their clients experienced the pandemic and what they did to thrive and overcome it.
- "Business Selling Insights" brought together business brokers to share their insights on what it takes to sell a business in today's market.
- "Exit Smart" brought together certified exit planning advisors from across the country, discussing how each serves their clients in preparing a business owner for transition.

Why Should You Participate in an Expert Anthology Book?

There are two reasons you should strongly consider being a part of an expert anthology book. First, it's possibly the fastest authorship method available to you. It's also the quickest way to get an author page on Amazon. Your prospects and clients can immediately see that you are a published author without waiting for your signature book to be completed. While crafting your sizzle book or signature book, you can enjoy the benefits of the instant authority your brand gets from having an author page on Amazon.

The second and probably more important reason why you should participate in an anthology book is for the marketing positioning that the book's third-party endorsement gives you.

When we published real estate agents in "Real Estate Insights" and certified exit planning advisors in "Exit Smart," we were telling the world that we recognized these ten people as leaders in their field. From the reader's perspective, this builds trust in these featured specialists.

A signature or sizzle book tells the world, "Here is who I am, and I hope you think I'm great." On the other hand, an anthology book tells the world that *others* believe you are great, and by "others," I am talking about the publisher or the platform.

What others say about you is more powerful than what you say about yourself. In my DJ coaching business, I invited ten of my best students to share how they make receptions unique. I published them in a book called "Remarkable Receptions." In another book, I published another group of students' contributions in "The Ultimate Wedding Reception."

Each of the books featured interview-style content just like a sizzle book, and in the book, I introduced these DJ entertainers as educators and advocates representing the best experts in their field. You see, they didn't have to say that they were experts. I, the interviewer, did it for them, and the book did it for them.

This type of book usually takes you less than fifteen minutes for the interview and less than thirty or forty minutes to approve or expand the edited manuscript. So, you can have a book on Amazon in less than an hour of your own time. Within weeks, your Amazon Author page will also become visible for the whole world to see. Ideally, you'll have this trifecta in your arsenal.

What Topics Should You Cover in an Anthology Book?

A common misconception is that in an anthology, each participant should cover a specific topic for their chapter. That is too limiting for all involved as more than one may want to be known for the same topic. Instead, the best format I have found for anthology books is the "professional spotlight." This allows each individual to discuss how *they* uniquely serve their clients. Because each participant has their own way of working with clients, their processes and stories will differ even if two professionals have the same specialty.

Another thing to consider is that this type of book is seldom read cover-to-cover. Instead, the readers typically make a beeline to read about the specific person they received the book from or were referred to.

Book Perspectives in Summary

Signature books create your identity in the world. Your signature book shows the world who you are, who you serve, and the core ways you serve them. It defines your greatest marketplace advantage; you gain a loyal following and leave a legacy.

Sizzle books are great for specialization. Your sizzle book gives people a bite-sized sample of your work, demonstrating micro-specializations with its "one problem, one solution" format.

An anthology book tells the world that others say you're great.

An anthology book gives you a fast track to authorship. It gets you on Amazon now, not later. It also gives you third-party endorsement and credibility of your expert status by placing you on a panel of experts.

With these three types of books, your Amazon Author page will look impressive, and you will have the key components of your Prime Positioning Portfolio.

KEY TAKEAWAYS

- Your signature book helps make your business' offerings stand apart from the competition. You don't want to suffer from "Google commoditization," where prospective customers lose you in a sea of competitors because you promote a common term. Instead, your signature book can create a new industry term that you can brand, so you are seen as the creator, and all searches for that new term lead to you.

- Publish a sizzle or "ask-the-expert" book to demonstrate your expertise within a narrow sub-specialty in your field. This "one problem, one solution" type of book lets your prospects know that you can address their specific problem with the proper expertise. This is the opposite of an "everything you needed to know about X" type of book.

- Participate in an anthology book, a group of interviews with other experts in your field because such books qualify you as an expert from a third-party perspective. Instead of vouching for your own expertise, the book's third-party positioning and "expert profiles" format give the impression that a third party is endorsing you, providing you with greater credibility.

CHAPTER TEN

Easy Authorship

*"If you really want to do something, you'll find a way.
If you don't, you'll find an excuse."*
— Jim Rohn

Publishing a book has never been faster or easier. It's no longer a mystery. The preconceived notions around publishing were created to block people from trying to join the "Published Author" club. In this chapter, I'll show you how the publishing world's doors have been opened to everyone, similar to how changes to the music industry have allowed anyone to get their music heard. Nowadays, books and music can be judged purely on their merits, not blocked by a false belief that you need to be chosen by some authoritative higher power. First, I'll demystify the intimidating process of writing a book. Then, I'll show you how simple the book creation process is and how you can finish an influential book quickly. Finally, I'll tell you how to enlist the help of others to get your book published fast.

Say Goodbye to Traditional Book Publishing Barriers

There was a time before the internet when many things were a mystery. The internet has exposed everything, and you could debate whether that's good news or not. Answers to these long-standing mysteries are a few keystrokes away on Google. Businesses can no longer get away with lousy service without risking bad reviews.

Well, writing books and getting published are two of the myths debunked by the web.

Do you remember record labels? I owned one in the 1980s called "House Nation Records."

Secret #1: Record Labels Figured Out How Easy It Was to Press Record and Keep Our Processes and Sources a Mystery Because We Didn't Want Competition

There was no internet back then, so our secret was pretty safe. Most ladders are run by people who aim to prevent your ambition to climb. Think about certifications, associations, organizations, etc. But that's another controversial topic for another book.

For the purpose of this book, understand that artists, just like authors, were being vetted by a tiny group of people who wanted to control the media. You could view this as some sort of censorship. Either way, labels propagated the concept that — if you wanted to speak, play music, or become visible in the music scene — you had to get their blessings.

Secret #2: Record Labels Wanted Artists Who Were Already Selling Something

There is a misconception that artists and writers are somehow discovered and raised from isolation in their basements, promoted to the masses, and made superstars. In reality, nothing could be further from the truth. Labels, just like publishers, want to take something from good to great instead of taking something that is nothing to something.

It's the same way today. The few record labels still in business are looking for artists that already show grit. These artists already show their ability to promote themselves. They're already doing shows locally and have built a small following. Labels want to know that you will hustle, and if you're already doing shows and gathering decent crowds, they will give you a closer look. Labels rarely consider a band without any news around them. Record labels don't listen to demo tapes in isolation and with no other evidence of success.

I remember receiving piles of demo tapes in the mail with absolutely nothing else. In a few rare cases, some would show up with photos of the group in action in nightclubs, entertaining crowds, and other social proof that they were making some waves. Those were the demo tapes that rose to the top of the pile.

The Gatekeepers Are Gone

Can you see how the secrets above gave power to a few companies in the music industry? They were able to put psychological barriers and control over creators and act as gatekeepers and censors. They allowed only the chosen few to be privileged enough to get published!

The psychological barriers that kept the music industry closed also ruled book publishing. Thanks to the internet, the exposure of all these mysteries has taken power away from big record labels and book publishers and put it in the hands of the artists and authors where it should be.

With social media, frauds are quickly found out. All it requires to be successful is an honest, ethical person who believes in educating consumers and advocating for their success. Genuinely being your authentic self and wanting to help your clients and audience is what can help you achieve your goals. In fact, the very book you're holding in your hand — professionally published, professionally designed, laid out in the paperback format that you're familiar with — looks like a duck, quacks like a duck, it is a duck.

Would it have mattered if this book was published by a label like Penguin or Simon & Schuster? Would you have even cared? For many, those names have zero bearing. Your clients absolutely won't care. They just want solutions to their problems.

Do you know which of your favorite artists were independently published and which were on major record labels? Do you know the names of those record labels? Do you care? Or do you just love their music? Do you know which bands were brought out from the trenches, formed in the streets, hustled, and raised up? Or which ones were built from the ground up using a formula like the Backstreet Boys or 'N Sync, put together and manufactured from scratch intentionally for marketing purposes?

Famous Books and Authors You May Not Have Known Were Self-Published

Some well-known books were self-published, and you may not have known or cared. Books like *Fifty Shades of Grey*, *The Martian*, *The Tale of Peter Rabbit*, *Rich Dad Poor Dad*, and *Legally Blonde* were all self-published, to name a few.

Consider this list of authors: Dan Kennedy, Beatrix Potter, Charles Dickens, Benjamin Franklin, Ernest Hemingway, Stephen King, Rudyard Kipling, James Patterson, Tom Peters, Edgar Allan Poe, J.K. Rowling, George Bernard Shaw, Henry David Thoreau, Leo Tolstoy, Mark Twain, and Walt Whitman.

Those famous names have self-published one or all of their books. You still know and love them. The one thing you should know about these self-published books is that they didn't allow someone to censor them. They had 100 percent creative freedom — which is precisely what you need when you want to help your audience!

Let's Begin Authoring Your Book

Who Is Your Audience?

To write an influential book, you must speak directly to your ideal prospect or client. Knowing your target audience deeply will help you develop your content and title. I want you to analyze your target audience carefully.

First, start by thinking of what industry your audience is in. Are you helping a business-to-business (B2B) audience? For example, are you working in a particular niche like accounting or health and wellness?

Next, please go one more layer deep and consider which niche within that industry you are serving. For example, if you're writing for people in the legal sector, which law niche do you write for? Perhaps it is family law. If you're writing for folks in health and wellness, nutrition is one niche, and weight loss is another.

Let's go one layer deeper. Who is your target audience within that niche, otherwise known as "your customer avatar?" In the family law example, perhaps you are writing for divorcing male or female business owners. This is a much more specific target audience. One example of specialization in action from a successful family law attorney is a TV commercial promoting a book called "Dad's Rights."

Pillow Talk / Kitchen Table Talk

> *"Always enter the conversation already taking place in the customer's mind."*
> *— Robert Collier*

What is the conversation that is already in your customer's mind? You can grab their attention powerfully by addressing the problems they are facing. You can demonstrate that you know them very well and let them know you understand the "pillow talk" that goes on when a husband and wife talk about their day as they hit the pillow. Or you can show your familiarity with the kinds of conversation they have at the kitchen table.

Imagine you were a fly on the wall to zero in on this information. What is it that you would hear? And could that conversation spark ideas for titles and headlines for your content? Is it something that speaks to those topics of conversation that suggests a better solution or path?

Your Table of Contents

Here, you will research to find what topics are already working and improve upon that list. The idea is not to reinvent the wheel but to offer improvements to the wheel and your unique perspectives about the wheel.

You will need to do a few things to put together a solid table of contents. First, go on Amazon and find best sellers that share the same category as the book you're going to publish. No, I'm not going to tell you to copy their table of contents, but I want you to see commonalities between these best-selling books' table of contents.

What was the smartest thing Burger King did when emerging in the market and researching locations? They looked at where all the McDonald's locations were and opened up across the street from them. If Burger King couldn't afford a store location research "A" team like McDonald's could; why wouldn't they simply go where McDonald's set up shop? McDonald's had already done Burger King's homework for them!

Write down the table of contents of several of the best-selling titles in your category. You're going to look for gaps in the content. Your next research step is to go to forums, message boards, and social media groups. Find out what your target audience is seeking. Find out what their burning questions are.

Next, look at the reviews of the books that you're using for research on Amazon. Look for common praises and common mistakes and complaints. Search for people who wished the author would have discussed this or that topic.

Take notes. This is where you have the opportunity to fill those best-selling books' gaps with your book. If you want to write a book between 100 to 150 pages, which I recommend, think about doing 7 to 10 chapters.

Don't hold yourself to any rigid structure, but if you look at each chapter being around 1,000 to 1,500 words, ten chapters will give you a 15,000-word book. This will put you between 100 to 140 pages, which is perfect for a signature book!

As a side note, I want to point out that people think books look hard to write because there are so many pages, but people do not realize it takes very little to fill those pages.

I also suggest you go to Audible.com and look at the books there. You are going to find that some of the most popular books range anywhere from only two-and-a-half to six hours of content. That's all! Two-and-a-half to six hours of polished writing is all it takes to have an excellent book. I will not oversimplify and make you think it is that easy. You still need two-and-a-half to six hours of good writing. Still, this is doable. The audio length of great books shows that book writing isn't as intimidating as people believe. This perception of difficulty works to your advantage since your competitors will be intimidated even to consider creating their own books in the first place!

Your Content

By this point, you should now have a rough idea of a table of contents to work from. Don't worry; the TOC may fluctuate a little bit as your books take on a life of their own.

Write down your TOC using simple 4 x 6 index cards, or if you prefer, digital devices like a Google Doc or project organization board like Trello.com. Write the title of your chapter on an individual index card, Trello board card, or line on Google Docs. Then, on the back of the index card or your Trello card, write down the 3 to 5 big ideas you want to express about that particular topic.

Your chapters are going to be very simple to create. You're going to start the chapter by telling people why this chapter is important and what they will learn from it, which gives them a reason to read on. If done correctly, it will intrigue them to read that chapter.

In the next part of the chapter, you're going to teach the 3 to 5 big ideas. Then at the end of that chapter, you will give them the key takeaways, which is a summary of what you just taught. This aligns with the tried and true teaching formula of telling people what you're going to teach them, teaching them, and then telling them what you just taught them.

Brevity

Your book's target rule of thumb should be around 80 to 150 pages. This is typically anywhere from 10,000 to 20,000 words. You can write just 1,000 words per topic if you have ten topics. This is doable since it's roughly the size of a typical article or blog post. Assuming you really hustle and focus on one topic per day, your book should be done in 10 days.

Of course, life happens, and the writing schedule above might be too optimistic. You might want to use one day for prep and one day for writing. Or, simply do one topic per week, just like a pastor, and then after a maximum of ten weeks, you could be done with your first draft.

How simple was that? To keep the chapters of your book brief and to the point, consider enlisting the help of a professional.

Get a Writing Partner, Friend, or Professional

While writing your individual chapters, you want to write them in an approachable and conversational way, as if you're teaching a friend, family member, or colleague. Teach and explain the topic to them in layman's terms so they can understand. The less they know about a subject initially, the better because you want them to be able to understand it clearly. This also helps ensure that you speak their language and not your industry's jargon.

Sometimes we forget this, speak over people's heads, and do not realize it. Essentially, this writing partner acts as the surrogate for your reader. They will be able to give you feedback on whether or not you are explaining things well. That will provide you with ideas for how to explain things more clearly.

Work with your chapter cards one topic at a time.

KEY TAKEAWAYS

- The internet has removed all traditional barriers to publishing. Many self-published authors go on to great success and fame since readers focus on quality, not a publishing house pedigree.
- Get into the heads of your target audience by thinking about the conversations they might be having in private. When your book's title and chapters speak in terms of your audience's 'pillow talk,' you are likely to get and keep their attention.
- Reverse engineer best-selling books that share your planned book's category. Figure out what they all have in common. Look for 'gaps' in their topic coverage. Read their reviews and be on the lookout for when commenters wished the book focused on a specific topic.
- Compile all your table of contents notes using a Google Doc or 4 x 6 index cards. Write the chapter topic on the front and the big 3 to 5 ideas on the back of the card.

- Run whatever you've written past a layman friend. They will let you know if you're using terms they either don't understand or assume too much. By having your friend review your text, your book will have the friendly advising tone it needs.

CHAPTER ELEVEN

Seven Steps to an Amazing Book

*"Either write something worth reading or
do something worth writing."*
— *Benjamin Franklin*

I n the previous chapter, we discussed planning and gathering your book angle ideas, specialized knowledge, and topics. Here is the action plan for getting your book done.

Step 1 - Write the Manuscript

Use this book's tips, tricks, and secrets to create your first draft manuscript. Don't worry if you don't consider yourself a good writer. Remember, people just want solutions to their problems. There are professionals who write for a living. They can take the ideas from your head and use your personality, including your jokes and personal '-isms' to ghostwrite your book. I don't want this step to hold you up. Focus on just getting your ideas down.

You can certainly contact my office if you're looking for a

professional writer to help you extract your ideas and get them to print for you. We do this for many executives who have absolutely zero time to write their own manuscript or don't feel confident about their writing. You shouldn't need a second career as a writer to have a successful book. That's what professional writers are for. Either way, get your manuscript done.

Step 2 - Proofreading Pass With Editing for Readability

Again, get professional help for this step because you cannot proofread your own work. You will rarely catch your own mistakes. Everything is going to make sense to you because you wrote it. But another set of eyes may be confused by what you wrote, and they will allow you to clarify. This proofreading step with editing helps improve your text's readability and boosts your intended readers' comprehension of your book's ideas.

Step 3 - Structure Improvement Pass

For this step, you need to read through the book several times.

In music, when we master a song, we do a process called "a mixdown." We will listen to the song and only focus on one track/instrument at a time. Let's say the song has 24 tracks and a whole bunch of them are just for the drums - bass drum, snare, three tom-toms, and several cymbals. The vocals can also take up several tracks. Then the bassline, guitars, synthesizers, or other instruments.

When we mix down a track, each time we listen to the song in its entirety, we focus only on one instrument at a time so we can build a balance we love. Often, we start with the kick drum and the bassline. We get that grooving; then we start bringing in additional passes. We bring in the other instruments to a level that accents the groove. We do it this way because it is nearly impossible to try balancing all the instruments simultaneously. You're bound to miss something. It is much more efficient to focus on one instrument at a time.

For this same reason, we go through a manuscript several times. This editing pass is for structure improvement. This step involves looking for ways to say things better. This step is all about clarity. Sometimes, steps 2 and 3 can happen in one pass.

Step 4 - Revisions From the Author

At this point, the author will be given the manuscript. This version will have structural improvements, minor changes, and edits done. This is where the author gets the chance to read through the draft manuscript thoroughly, ensuring their ideas remain clear and accurately communicated in the draft. They also have the opportunity to add any (perhaps minor) clarifications or any ideas they might have missed initially. Be careful at this stage! An artist can literally change their art endlessly, forever. Stay on point, and don't make this mistake!

Step 5 - Incorporating the Revisions From the Author

Once the author has revised each chapter, it goes back to the editor. The editor takes those revisions from the author and does another pass of proofreading and revisions. This time around, the editor focuses solely on the changes requested by the author.

Step 6 - Clarity Editing Pass

In this phase, the editor is looking for opportunities for supporting side notes. The editor looks to see if a case study could help clarify a point or whether a checklist can help. The editor is looking for any big ideas and improvements to put a final polish on your book.

Step 7 - Final Elements Editing

In the "final elements" pass, we will find places to add your testimonials; just three to five is good. You don't want to overdo it because your book might look 'salesy.'

We're also looking for opportunities to add a call to action and cross-promotion in this pass. Can you promote another book of yours in a section that discusses a topic your other book covers? Maybe your text presents opportunities to cross-promote different types of programs you offer with a call to action. Again, be careful not to overdo it since you don't want to risk your book looking salesy.

Step 7 is also where we figure out which "engagement devices" would be helpful and where to place them in the book. For example, adding an engagement device early in the book is always a good tip.

Many people who open books never get to finish them. To address this, get your readers to a webpage with a form to enter their name and email. You can send them a checklist (or another valuable piece of information) that can help extend their attention to the subject of your book.

Another reason we do this is that not all books will be purchased directly from you. Amazon, for example, does not share your book's buyer list or their information. You won't know the contact information of the people who bought your book on Amazon. Including a call to action that leads to your email collection page is an excellent way of working around Amazon not disclosing your book's buyer contact info.

These seven amazing steps help you create a killer signature book that you will use for years to come. Perhaps it can even define your entire career! One book can launch you to millions.

Formats

Print

Let me be clear: Print books are mandatory. Nothing beats a physical book. With everything going digital these days, although it may be tempting, I do not advise you to go that route. Why? Because if you haven't noticed, PDFs and digital files go out of sight, out of mind quickly. People already forget them seconds after they've requested them.

I can't tell you how many PDFs I've been encouraged to download and quickly forgotten about within an hour of saving the file to my hard drive or phone. Who goes into their hard drive and digs up forgotten files? Nobody!

What you want is the "visual factor." You want that book staring at people, even sitting on their desks or tables. Physical books give you the "pass-along factor." People will remember a book. They will see it constantly even if they don't read it at the time. It's always there as a reminder that it exists for when they are ready to use it. A physical book always reminds your prospects about the solutions the book solves. So, when your prospective customer's friend or colleague has a problem that the book solves, your prospective client will think or say, "Oh, yeah! I've got a book about that. Let me loan it to you." You can't loan a Kindle book.

Physical books give you the "autograph factor." You can subtly use that local celebrity factor and autograph your book as people would expect you to do at dinner seminars and events.

Books possess that "tangible factor." Studies have been done on the decline of music sales and artists' fan bases due to the digitization of music. Album covers were created for deeper engagement with listeners, and they nurtured people into raving fans. People would buy the albums. They would stare at the covers and read and study the covers inside and out while listening to the music. When things went digital, and album design and art were reduced to tiny, useless thumbnails, artists lost an integral tool they needed for connecting with and cultivating fans.

Don't let this happen with your books!

You also want a paperback so you can control distribution and list building. For example, if you do speaking engagements, your books can play a vital part in your success. First of all, the reason that they invited you to speak about your title and your book already pre-defines you to that speaking event's audience. It also allows you to gift the book. The event promoter can even purchase books for every attendee at a conference. Physical books will enable you to sign autographs and create a greater sense of status, personal connection, and perceived authority.

Physical books are priceless. As mentioned, you can control your list building because Amazon doesn't share your book's buyer list. To get around this, you can offer your physical book at a special sale if your audience purchases directly from you on your website. That way, you're controlling your list building. You can run lead-generating ads perpetually to your books. This creates an entry door to your business.

You will feel safe and secure when you keep physical copies handy at all times in your briefcase and car. You might be sitting on an airplane, and the person next to you asks you what you do. You can hand them a copy of your book and politely excuse yourself to go to the bathroom. Who knows? Maybe that person could really use you. Can you see how a physical book makes a great conversation starter?

Kindle

Although I just ranted about making sure you have a print paperback book, I want you also to offer a Kindle version. This allows you to gain the maximum benefit of search results on Amazon when you are in both paperback and Kindle versions. Also, having a Kindle version will enable you to offer flash sales for less than the print cost of a paperback. It is harder to do this when you have to cover your book's printing cost.

Kindle requires a Kindle reader app on the reader's phone or device. Even though it's not great, some people will still prefer Kindle, so you can serve them too. It simply allows those who prefer Kindle to have that option. Still, having a print paperback available allows you to enjoy all the powerful benefits of your reader's ability to hold your tangible book in their hand and let the cover art anchor your brand in their mind.

Digital Flipbook

I'll say it again: I want you to have a paperback. Still, you can use a digital flipbook for lead-generation purposes. One of the coolest things we provide our clients is a digital flipbook version of their book. What's cool about it is that it looks exactly like the physical book but on the computer screen. In fact, when you swipe a page with your mouse, it makes the turning pages sound, and the book actually flips over. You can read it cover to cover, flipping through every page all the way to the back. It still beats a PDF because it makes the book come alive and look like a physical book.

Sampling is something cool you can do with these flipbooks that we help clients with. You can peel out just one chapter of your book as a free preview, so perhaps you can use a lead-generating ad or a button on your website that says, "Download Chapter 1 of (this book)." You can create a flipbook that has the front and back cover but only the first chapter for sampling. This method helps you control lead generation because, again, Amazon doesn't share their buyer info with you.

Publish and Profit

Many companies offer book printing services. You can use companies like Lulu.com, 48hrbooks.com, or Lightning-Press.com if you're just interested in printing books. We help our clients set up their books on Amazon, Kindle, and expanded distribution to other fine booksellers if they want the whole online publishing package. They get paid directly from Amazon and keep 100% of the royalties. We help them get completely set up and be seen as Amazon authors. This includes registering them to claim their Amazon author pages. When our clients' prospective customers type their names in Google, they often see our clients' author page as a top result. Amazon has such a high domain authority that its pages — including author pages — rank highly on Google search results, often higher than our client's websites.

Imagine your prospects, clients, and referrals first seeing your Amazon author page. Imagine your prospects quickly discovering that you are a published author and have "written the book" on the very subject that they want help with. How's that for separating you instantly from the competition? How's that for INSTANT AUTHORITY?

KEY TAKEAWAYS

- Prioritize the physical print version of your signature book. This format helps ensure your brand stays top of mind to your prospects, while digital books like PDFs are often quickly downloaded and forgotten. Physical books stand as constant reminders of your expertise.
- Physical books can lead to referrals when your prospects pass them on to people they know who can use your expertise.
- Physical books supplement your attendance at speaking events and help cement your status as an authority.

- You should still publish a Kindle version of your book, so your name appears on search engines.
- Get a digital flipbook version of your book to maximize your online exposure and reach your target audience to build your mailing list regardless of their format preferences.
- We offer a complete publishing package so clients can be paid directly from Amazon and quickly get an author page that ranks high on Google. This gives them a competitive advantage when their prospective customers look them up on Google to see they are the published authority on their prospects' problems.

CHAPTER TWELVE

Mo' Money: Advanced Business Ideas for Your Book

"Almost anyone can be an author; the business is to collect money and fame from this state of being."
— A. A. Milne

I f you've made it this far, you already know everything you need to craft an influential client-grabbing book. This chapter will show you other strategies that can exponentially extend your book's reach. I'll also cover methods you can use to repurpose your book's content.

The Book License

Are you a coach in your industry, or have you considered becoming one as a side hustle? Maybe you've thought of building a coaching business or switching to a coaching career. If any of the above apply to you, you can license your consumer or B2B-facing book to peers who want to achieve what you have achieved.

From 1994 to 2012, I owned a DJ entertainment service that performed regularly at weddings, bar mitzvahs, and corporate events in the Chicagoland area. I knew I wanted to transition out of that business. When I learned about information marketing from my mentor Dan Kennedy, I took everything I knew about growing my DJ business using direct response marketing and packaged it into a paid course that I called "DJs Edge." In 2005, I started running ads in DJ trade magazines offering this course, and I started coaching other DJs. I repurposed all of my existing marketing materials, and I licensed all of my marketing materials to members of my coaching program. I'm proud that my course has allowed many of my thousands of students to take their businesses from a money-spending hobby to over six figures, with one of my members growing from six to seven figures per year using my system.

Eventually, I licensed my book to my coaching members. Now I have licensees in the USA and Canada. This was the same wedding reception DJ book I used to give brides to attract clients. All I did was allow my coaching students to use my book to improve their local businesses around the country using a strict area-exclusive license system. This way, only one DJ can use my book per city.

Each license enables members to list their name as a co-author and their photo on the cover. Their custom book also contains a chapter featuring their exclusive interview. Each member pays a set of license fees plus an annual renewal to keep their territory. Customized books give them instant credibility.

You could consider doing this with your book immediately or in the future, depending on how you feel about competition, whether you need protected territories, or whether you have an abundance mindset. You can get a fee and recurring passive income if you custom license your book.

Nato Guajardo is one of several clients I've helped license out books for passive recurring revenue. Nato is in the property and casualty insurance coaching business. In his insurance practice, business is mostly driven by referrals from mortgage loan officers.

He coaches other P&C insurance agencies on how to get referrals the same way he does.

He sends a book to mortgage loan originators that teaches them how to generate home buyer leads. His mortgage broker-facing book is *Ask Nato Guajardo: What You Need to Know About Generating Exclusive Home Buyer Leads With Good Credit So You Can Close More Loans Fast.* As you can imagine from the title, these books are magnetic to mortgage professionals because the title speaks to their aspirations.

When they receive the book, the book shows the MLO the premise of how to run inexpensive social media ads to generate inbound leads. In the book, the insurance agent offers to set up the entire system for the mortgage loan originator for free. This starts a referral-partner relationship between the MLO and the insurance agent. Whenever the insurance agent helps more mortgage brokers generate home buyer leads, the mortgage broker is naturally inclined to return the favor by passing along insurance referrals to the insurance agent that helped them generate the home buyer leads in the first place.

For Nato, he created the book once, used it in his own practice, and then offered to license it to his coaching members so they could use it, generating referrals for his members and generating additional revenues for his coaching business. At this point, Nato can offer this book to his members in many different ways. He can bundle the license with his highest-paying membership level, where his highest-paying coaching members can use the book in their territory as long as they remain members. Or, Nato can choose to offer the high-ticket license a la carte along with a monthly or annual renewal fee.

In both our cases, we took our existing book assets and gained additional revenue from licensing. You can choose to take this route from the very beginning so you can liquidate all your original publishing costs. It's like being paid to create the asset and then using it for free.

The Inner Circle Book Concept

The idea behind the inner circle concept (also known as the round-table) is to gather all your referral partners to discuss a theme. For example, I picked ten people from different industries and had them discuss how they marketed their businesses. This was in my Dan Kennedy Mastermind group. I used this bonus to provide extra value to the members' subscriptions. Plus, I could use the completed program to attract more new members into the group by letting people eavesdrop or listen in on conversations about marketing from a very high-level group where they shared some excellent secrets on what they're doing to grow their businesses.

The theme of the book was "mastermind marketing methods." It taught the reader how to identify breakthrough ideas their industry hasn't seen before by finding and repurposing innovations outside their industry. An example of this concept in action is how the drive-through window expanded from banks to fast food restaurants. Drive-through windows so thoroughly revolutionized banking and fast food that there's controversy about who copied who.

Not only can the roundtable book method create an asset that your subscription group members can use, but all participants who helped in its creation can also use the book in their marketing efforts. In fact, there's a strong incentive for folks to participate in creating the book. They're all contributing to baking a cake they get to eat later.

This tactic could be part of a local networking group like BNI (Business Network International). Any complementary, noncompetitive inner circle or mastermind group could use this method. This method creates fast authorship for all involved. All the conversations can simply be taken from a group recording, transcribed, edited, and published in print paperback form.

This is why I love books.

They're so flexible, and there are so many creative marketing strategies you can execute with books. Books are appealing and attractive. It's easy to gain cooperation from many folks with whom you'd like to create relationships just by mentioning that you're publishing a book and would love their contribution.

KEY TAKEAWAYS

- In addition to helping you land more customers and clients with a book that makes customer acquisition more effortless, you should consider licensing your book for other professionals like you to use in their respective markets.
- License your book to other complementary businesses in your field that serve the same client or customer. (Example: DJ Book is licensed by a wedding planner to give to their clients).
- Collaborate with experts in other fields around a common theme to produce an "Inner Circle" book that pools all your expertise. Use this book as a free premium that adds value to whatever coaching or membership program you run. This book effectively cross-promotes each participant's business to the various audiences it reaches.

CHAPTER THIRTEEN

How My Team Can Create Your Kickass Book

"Start before you're ready."
— Steven Pressfield, *The War of Art*

You just discovered all the powerful ways a book can catapult your career and distinguish your brand for a lifetime. Although I've demystified book creation for you, there's still some work involved. But the good news is that you don't have to do it alone.

How would you like to author your book with your personality and ideas without writing a single word? How would you like to complete your book within a few weeks and dedicate just a couple of hours of your own time? Or maybe you have already written a manuscript but need help taking it to the finish line? Do you have existing videos, blog articles, or perhaps a speech that contains all the content you want in your book?

In this chapter, you'll see the range of ways that my team can turn your ideas and knowledge into your signature book. We even have existing content in several professional fields that you can simply license in the form of a private label. You only need to add your name to our existing private label book. On the other hand, my professional ghost-writing team can write a custom book from scratch without you having to write a single word. All you need to do is talk to my writing team.

We Can Craft Your Book From Your Existing Content

Do you have a video series or a YouTube channel with various videos on different topics that can be organized into individual chapters for a book? Do you have a webinar you teach? Do you have a series of articles or blog posts? Maybe you have an online course?

Many folks don't realize that if you have any of the above, you already have the makings of a book. Did you know that many books started as live training events, high-ticket seminars, or courses taught in person? Authors simply boiled down whatever instructional content they already had to produce their books.

Imagine a $2,000 or $3,000 seminar turned into a book that somebody can purchase for less than $20. It happens all the time, and people don't realize that these books can become the foundation for their careers. You, too, can build your career on the solid foundation laid out by your existing course materials or content.

Dan Kennedy did this with his book *The Ultimate Sales Letter* and his second book, *The Ultimate Marketing Plan.* Dan explained that these books started as multi-thousand-dollar live training programs at an early seminar. Later, these became the foundation of his career as an author, and he went on to make millions based on work derived from those books.

In the case of a YouTube channel, the video content just has to be organized by topic in a way that makes sense for your reader to digest. Of course, the videos most likely relay information logically and sequentially. You only need to transcribe the content from videos into first-person prose.

You can have a book in no time by just turning over this content to my team!

We Can Craft Your Book From Your Own Written Manuscript

Do you like to write? Even if you don't consider yourself a good writer, we can polish your manuscript by keeping your voice and personality intact while ensuring your book is professionally written. This involves checking for and fixing grammar mistakes and proofreading for style and clarity. It doesn't matter if you think you're the worst writer in the world. If you can speak to teach somebody a concept —as if you're training a staff member or a friend — you can get these instructions down on paper. We'll then clean up and tighten your text.

You could even record these instructions and turn the recording over to our writers. Professional writing is a second career; you don't need to do it. Please stick to your core competency, and leave the writing to us.

We Offer Complete Ghostwriting Services From Scratch

We specialize in working with busy professionals, executives, and business owners who want their books written fast without having to write a single word. This is our most popular program.

We start with a Book Discovery video meeting where we work with you to clarify your target audience and objectives for the book. We help you develop your content plan and table of contents. We'll then schedule short 15 to 30-minute book chats via phone or video meeting to extract your knowledge and ideas through simple questions you can readily answer. We'll transcribe and edit these sessions to produce one to two book chapters per session.

In these sessions, you simply answer our questions regarding your chapter's topic. The meeting is recorded, and our writing team transcribes, writes, and edits the audio interview into a chapter or two of your book. Your book's prose will be written in first-person and reflect your personality. This means your expressions, communication styles, and verbal mannerisms are included. Once we transcribe, edit, and proof, we'll send you your book's manuscript draft to tweak, revise, or approve as you see fit.

I'm proud of my team of writers, editors, proofreaders, formatters, and designers who do a tremendous job turning client ideas and knowledge into their very own signature book. It is surreal to read Amazon reviews of books we have ghostwritten for clients where readers comment on their love of the author's personality, expressions, and mannerisms.

We have a wide range of book-authoring programs to accommodate your needs — from finishing and publishing any existing manuscript to strategizing and crafting your book from scratch. We can also extract book chapters from whatever existing content you may already have or interview you so you can dictate your book chapter by chapter.

Working with a publishing service should be easy, and there should be no extra charges or upsells. Unlike other companies, I specialize in a no-surprises, easy, transparent quote, so you can feel secure knowing there will never be any hidden fees, upsells, or unexpected charges.

Our wide range of content creation services ensures nothing will get in the way of you becoming a published author in your field. Let's get started!

Here's What to Do Next:

1. Schedule a **"Book Discovery Call"** with us at **www.BooksGrowBusiness.com**.
2. Let us recommend and execute an action plan for your business.
3. Use your book to grow your name recognition, authority, and profits!

Then, Do This When You Have Your Book:

1. Send books to all your prospects, past clients, and peers.
2. Promote your book before your services, so you are seen as an advocate (not a salesperson).
3. Use your book as your daily playbook for content year-round.
4. Perpetually attract new clients that pay, stay, and refer!

KEY TAKEAWAYS

- My company offers fast, expert self-publishing options for authors regardless of the materials you have already created for your potential book (if any).
- We can help you get published quickly by repurposing existing webinars, blog posts, videos, or online course materials you have already created.
- We can edit, reorganize, supplement, and edit your existing manuscript so you can become a published author faster.
- We can interview you to produce a book that best fits your personality and personal communication style. This option helps you craft your book from scratch.
- Schedule a call with us; we will give you a plan, then use your book to grow your business.
- Send copies of your book to past and present clients and peers.
- Use your book for year-round content inspiration.

Complimentary Book Discovery Session

Would you like **FREE** help with your book idea? Or do you need an idea for a book that will attract your ideal clients?

Schedule your complimentary, no-obligation 30-minute **"Book Discovery Session"** at the link below to connect with my team and me.

Together, we will explore your goals and ideas, and create a clear action plan to get an excellent book done fast that brings you the clients of your dreams.

Visit: www.BooksGrowBusiness.com

CHAPTER FOURTEEN

BONUS Interview with Chief Editor, Shannon Buritz

The key to a great book is getting professional help. You can focus on what ideas you want to share. At the same time, a professional writer and editor will be sure your ideas are presented in the most attractive, clear, and compelling way while expressing your style and personality. In this bonus chapter, you'll read an interview with my Chief Editor, Shannon Buritz, who will share her system for creating your signature book.

Please tell us a little about your work and the types of clients you help.

Shannon Buritz: As a professional ghostwriter and editor for Remarkable Press, I help busy professionals complete their books efficiently, from the outline to the published product. At Remarkable Press, we have published over 500 professionals, helping them achieve the distinction of Published Author, with an Author Page on Amazon. Many of our clients have received Best-Seller status for their work. This is incredibly valuable when prospects perform due diligence on our clients and find their Amazon author page appears at the top of their Google search. We specialize in working with business owners and self-employed professionals, including, but not limited to, financial advisors, exit planners, business brokers, divorce attorneys, business coaches, and DJ entertainers. We have even published dog trainers and pest control experts, helping them stand out amongst their competition.

What is the biggest challenge your clients commonly face regarding authoring a book?

Shannon Buritz: The challenge is twofold. First, many busy professionals consider writing a book a daunting, time-consuming task. Many of our clients have an entire book inside their heads and just haven't gotten around to putting it all down on paper.

Second, many of our clients know their business inside and out but are less confident about their grammar and punctuation skills. They often don't know where to seek help to polish their ideas into a flowing, well-written manuscript.

How do you help them overcome this challenge?

Shannon Buritz: Our interview-style process extracts the content from their head using a conversational, stress-free method. We often liken it to "chatting over a beer." Our clients are pleasantly surprised to find they only need to devote a few hours of their own time to the content extraction process. We handle the rest, including writing, editing, formatting, cover design, publishing, and best-seller drive marketing campaigns. Our books are known for their eye-catching cover designs and titles, as the founder of

Remarkable Press, Mark Imperial, is a Dan Kennedy-trained and certified marketing genius.

What are some of the biggest mistakes or pitfalls you've seen people make when authoring a book?

Shannon Buritz: It is common for people to "overthink" when writing a book. In reality, you are the expert. All the knowledge, experience, and war stories are in your head, just waiting to be shared.

When you speak to your clients and prospects one-on-one, you are already doing the equivalent of writing a book. You are explaining solutions to their problems and answering their most pressing questions. With our proprietary method, we help you transfer that same experience into print! When you have your book, you gain the leverage of reaching an unlimited number of potential prospects (your readers), with your message delivered in perfect pitch every time.

Another big mistake people make when overthinking their book is attempting to write an epic "Everything You Need to Know" A to Z book about their subject, which is actually the worst thing to do if you want to have a book that attracts clients. Overdone books often turn out like textbooks and are unappealing. Instead, create an attractive book that appeals to readers by addressing their most significant challenges or desires. When we show clients this concept, they get excited because not only is that a much easier book to create, but also more fun!

We are here to prove to you that *anyone* can be an author. Just leave the technical aspects of writing to us and embrace what you know and what makes you unique and appealing to your prospects.

What inspired you to become a writer and editor? How did you get started?

Shannon Buritz: I graduated from Aurora University with a Bachelor's in Psychology in 2005. I spent my first years out of college in Case Management working for the State of Illinois. Much of my work involved report writing to help my clients reach their developmental goals. I have always had a passion for helping people and a knack for expressing ideas through the written word. I've also written Forensic reports used in court to prove guilt or innocence. Whether I like to admit it or not, I'm in the "marketing business!"

Becoming the Chief Editor for Remarkable Press has allowed me to touch the lives of hundreds of professionals. I love being part of their journey and seeing them reap the benefits of having a published book through speaking engagements, increased sales, and overall business growth.

Is there anything I didn't think to ask you that you would like to share with professionals considering authorship?

Shannon Buritz: Our mission is to get the word out to business professionals in every niche about the extensive list of benefits of being a published author. When faced with a guy who has a book and a guy who doesn't, a potential client will always choose the book guy. We make it an accessible way to gain instant credibility and recognition.

The number one obstacle to getting a book written and published is "intimidation," and we take that word out of the equation when you work with us. Whether you fear the time involved or your perceived lackluster vocabulary, we've got you covered.

Books grow business. It's really as simple as that.

If a business professional would like your
help authoring their book, how can they find
you, connect with you, and learn more?

Shannon Buritz: You can connect with us on our website: **www.
booksgrowbusiness.com.** We look forward to publishing you!

Shannon Buritz

Chief Editor, Remarkable Press

Graduating summa cum laude from Aurora University in 2005, Shannon earned her Bachelor's degree in Psychology and subsequently embarked on a career in Case Management with the State of Illinois. Here, her writing talent shone as she crafted detailed reports to aid clients in achieving developmental milestones, even drafting forensic reports instrumental in court proceedings.

Shannon's enthusiasm for aiding others and her innate ability to articulate complex ideas through writing soon found a new outlet. Today, she is the esteemed Chief Editor at Remarkable Press, a role she revels in. She has assisted more than 600 busy entrepreneurs in becoming published authors, enabling them to impart wisdom, accelerate business growth, and leave enduring legacies.

Shannon's life outside her profession is equally vibrant, living in Chicago's western suburbs. She shares her home with her soulmate, Mark, her lively children, Max and Felix, and an unconventional trio of pets - a turtle, a bearded dragon, and a French Bulldog named Fortune. When Shannon's pen is at rest, you can find her racking up miles on her bicycle, getting blank stares from her kids when making any request for assistance, watching scary movies, adventuring on road trips, and *not* cooking.

WEBSITE: www.booksgrowbusiness.com

Epilogue

"Every success story is a tale of constant adaptation, revision, and change."
— *Richard Branson*

Congratulations! You have just been transferred the essential knowledge you need to craft a powerful, influential book that can instantly catapult you to the top of your field. I say "instantly" because authority is instant when it is used. People immediately view you as an authority in the field when you have a book. That's because, whether you know it or not, you are! If this is your first book, you may not have claimed your authority card until now!

With your signature book, you have transformed yourself from a member of the mediocre majority with a business card (viewed as a salesperson) to the educator/advocate/obvious expert who "wrote the book" on your subject.

Too many folks will go through their entire career without a book, doing everything the hard way and going to great lengths to tell people who they are. It can be time-consuming to follow up and build trust, and this often ends up looking like salesperson behavior. It's like driving down the street with one foot on the gas and the other on the brake. All this heavy lifting can be done instantly with your signature book and the authority, credibility, and trust immediately linked to it.

Let us give you a signature book game plan. Then, you can go forth and create your book fast. We are here to help you in any area you desire.

Your signature book will be the nucleus of your business and personal brand. With it, you'll have the master key to fast acceptance. Clients will come to you more readily. Referrals will begin to flow. You will mingle with other influencers who can accelerate your notoriety and success. Your business will grow.

You'll reach people around the globe, transform lives with your ideas, and impact people positively. Your book can become the basis of all your brand messaging, including a podcast, YouTube channel, and email marketing campaign, to name a few.

I have a principle that I choose to live by, and I believe if you adopt this value, you will live a life of abundance. The principle is, "I choose to deliver value to the world worth 10x to 100x what I ask for or get in return."

If everyone lived with that mindset, would you agree that the world would be better? So go forth, get your books done, help as many people as possible with your gifts, and achieve your dreams!

Complimentary Book Discovery Session

Would you like **FREE** help with your book idea? Or do you need an idea for a book that will attract your ideal clients?

Schedule your complimentary, no-obligation 30-minute **"Book Discovery Session"** at the link below to connect with my team and me.

Together, we will explore your goals and ideas, and create a clear action plan to get an excellent book done fast that brings you the clients of your dreams.

Visit: www.BooksGrowBusiness.com

About the Author

MARK IMPERIAL is a best-selling author who learned the art of influential writing through his work with Dan S. Kennedy. He was one of the chosen few that Dan personally certified as an Independent Business Advisor in 2008. Mark has gone on to help over 500 professionals publish their client-attracting books in fields like Financial Planning, Family Law, Elder Law, and Business Exit Planning, to name a few.

Mark discovered the power of books that sell things when he wrote a pet iguana care book that sold over 50 iguanas every Sunday at a flea market, yielding $1,500+ before noon. He repeated that success by writing a wedding entertainment book that attracted clients to his DJ service and booked it solid year after year. This inspired Mark to share his love of crafting authority-defining books with business owners and professionals worldwide.

Currently residing in the western suburbs of Chicago, Mark shares his home with the love of his life Shannon, bonus children Max and Felix (who he affectionately refers to as "the chuckleheads"), a turtle, a bearded dragon, and Fortune, his beloved French Bulldog. When Mark isn't being a marketing nerd, he practices martial arts, keeps up with Shannon on her bicycle, eats Thai food, and watches his favorite TV show—infomercials. Visit: www.BooksGrowBusiness.com for more.

Testimonials

ADAM MARBURGER -
Author of "You're The F*cking Problem"

"You were able to help me complete the book and get it to market. So without you, my friend, I wouldn't be here, and I'm thankful. You were very professional. And you were very, very easy to work with. I mean, you made it frictionless. Well, first of all, the results are crazy. The book hit multiple best-selling categories. My inbox is flooded with opportunities. Over the last three weeks, I landed multiple speaking engagements - one internationally and a keynote in the Bahamas, Atlanta, Georgia, Caesar's Palace, and Vegas. Opportunities are everywhere now. And I almost feel I should write you into my will! But really, the best part is those who have already read the book and given me the feedback. I've changed so many lives, the messages that I get. I feel so great that I'm helping so many people, and the monetary stuff that comes from it, like the speaking gigs and the business, is all icing on the cake. It really is because of the joy I'm receiving from all of the lives I've touched; oh my goodness, gracious; it's a blessing. Mark and his team will make it really, really easy. They do the heavy lifting. Your reputation speaks for itself. Your professionalism speaks for itself. You've been doing this for a long time. And you did everything you said you were going to do. There was never a moment of gray area. It was black and white. You were super professional. Your team was super professional. You were punctual and professional and frickin' knocked it out of the park. Period."

JEREMY ACQUILANO -
Author of "Unsellable to Sold"

"My name is Jeremy Acquilano; I'm a business broker in Daytona Beach, Florida. I had this business expo that was coming up, and writing this book was just a lot to try and do in a short period of time. You know, I had about two months at the time that I decided to write a book. And it was really kind of a hassle trying to get everything down in such a short time. It was actually a big doubt in my mind that I could get it done.

The fact that I had a publisher in mind now was a huge motivation; it was like a huge hurdle out of the way. And then, when you explained that you guys do a little bit of ghostwriting, you guys offer the ability to ask me questions, and I can speak it out. And you guys could just jot everything down and write it for me; that really kicked me into gear, and I realized, okay, this can get done. So it gave me the hope that we could finish it in time.

It was a pleasure to talk with you guys and to be able to share everything with you. And then, you gave me some pointers on different things that I should include or shouldn't include in the book. And it gave me the right direction to ensure I was on time.

You guys over delivered on everything. You guys beat all the deadlines for everything. I got the book in hand last weekend, and I still have a week left until I actually need it. So we finished ahead of time. It was just a pleasure working with you guys."

PEGGY HOYT - Author of "All My Children
Wear Fur Coats," among other books

"Hi, my name is Peggy Hoyt. And I'm an estate planning and elder law attorney and now a best-selling author. I live in Central Florida, and I practice at the Law Offices of Hoyt and Bryant. I'm passionate about pets. And I host a weekly podcast that I call a pawcast titled All My Children Wear Fur Coats.

I was able to participate in one of your anthology book projects. And that was easy to do, fun and super simple, and a great way to get started in the book marketing business. But I had already accumulated a little stable of books of my own. And some of them were going stale. And I really needed to get them updated, get a fresh view, a fresh look, some fresh marketing. And that's where our relationship really blossomed because I was able to say to you, "Hey, Mark, I need help. And can you put the fire behind me to get me motivated to update these books? Give them a new good look, and get them out on the market?" And, of course, your answer was, "Absolutely, I can do that." And then, one day, I just had a crazy idea. I was like, "I'm going to write a book called 101 ways to F*ck Up Your Estate." And I told you about the idea, and you said, "I don't really like the title." But I said, "I don't care. I'm going to do it anyway; I just need your support." You said, "Absolutely. I'll give you my support." I was able to crank it out, get it out there. And that's the one that recently became a bestseller on Amazon.

Really, you motivate me more than I would motivate myself. So it is great having Mark as a partner because he nudges you to get you to do the things you need to do. I still owe you some content at the moment on another project that we're working on. But I will get it; I promise this weekend. So working together has been great because you laid out the format, the expectations for what we're going to do, the steps in the process, and what I need to do. Then as I complete my part of that process, I get feedback from your team. "So here's the next step. I need you to review this, edit this, and then submit the rest of this." And then it's all digital, or we do face-to-face video meetings, which is a lot of fun. But a lot of it is digital, so that you can do it from anywhere. And it just makes the whole thing seamless. So easy from start to finish on this last book. I bet it didn't even take three months.

There was a cover design process. So some ideas were presented for covers, and I couldn't get my arms around the original designs and shared some of them with my friends. I was using them as a kind of focus group. And then I came back with some suggestions and other ideas, and you came back with a new set of recommendations. And that worked out perfectly. And that did result in the cover that we have today, which is absolutely fabulous. Because it's so bright and eye-popping, and everybody loves it. But that was perfect because it made it easy to get the cover done. I sent you all of the content on a chapter-by-chapter basis. And then your team laid out all of the interior design. To me, that's the hardest part. I have done numerous books in the past, and getting the cover design and interior design was always a huge challenge for me. Having your team review and edit and ensure that I didn't misspell words was also an excellent part of the process. Once all of that was complete, I didn't have to do anything else. I just had to wait for the final product. You sent me a preview of the product. Once I okayed that final preview, boom, it went up on Amazon. And then I said, "How do we make this a best seller?" And we got busy, and we got it done.

I wish I'd had you for my first book! Because when I did my first one, I tried to pull all the pieces together myself. And it just was overwhelming. And you make a lot of false starts and go down some bunny trails, and you don't know how to get an ISBN, and you don't know how to find a cover designer, and you don't know how to find somebody to help design the interior. And you don't know how to find somebody to help edit the book, and you don't have this nice digital platform to work on. It was just a lot.

I would absolutely give my 100% raving review endorsement of Mark and his team. I didn't know him from Adam either when I met him, but I really liked him. And I've done a couple of projects now. And would highly, highly recommend you and your team. And if anybody has an idea for a book, and everybody does, we're all authors inside our hearts, right? So if you have an idea for a book, if you have a business you want to grow, writing a book is the best third-party credibility you're ever going to have."

Made in USA - Kendallville, IN
11949_9781954757288
10.02.2023 1347